just a little too thin

just a little too thin

*How to Pull Your Child Back
from the Brink of an Eating Disorder*

MICHAEL STROBER, PH.D.
MEG SCHNEIDER, MA, LMSW

Da Capo

LIFE
LONG
A Member of the
Perseus Books Group

Printed in the United States of America.

Da Capo Press is a member of the Perseus Books Group

Visit us on the World Wide Web at http://www.perseusbooks.com

Da Capo Press books are available at special discounts for bulk purchases in the United States by corporations, institutions, and other organizations. For more information, please contact the Special Markets Department:

Special Markets Department
Perseus Books Group
11 Cambridge Center
Cambridge, MA 02142
(800) 255–1514; (617) 252-5298
special.markets@perseusbooks.com

ISBN 0-7382-1018-8
ISBN 13: 978-0-7382-1018-6

A CIP record for this book is available from the Library of Congress.

05 06 07 / 10 9 8 7 6 5 4 3 2 1

To my wife, Courtney
For mystery, adventure, and wisdom

MS

To the Richard

MFS

CONTENTS

ACKNOWLEDGMENTS

During thirty years of professional life, one gains many friends and colleagues, infinitely generous with their support and advice, from whom much is learned. I have benefited greatly from their wit, intellect, and clinical insights, and I am grateful for a continuing working relationship with many, especially Drs. Cynthia Bulik, Ruth Striegel-Moore, Timothy Walsh, Craig Johnson, Allan Kaplan, Blake Woodside, Walter Kaye, James Mitchell, Katherine Halmi, Stephen Wonderlich, Harry Brandt, David Feinberg, Charles Portney, David Rudnick, Carol Edelstein, Harry Brandt, Manfred Fichter, Bernie Devlin, Kelly Klump, Pamela Keel, and Wade Berrettini. I am indebted to many others in the field of eating disorders whose research and clinical work have contributed in important ways to my learning, in particular Drs. Christopher Fairburn, Howard Steiger, Joel Yager, G. Terence Wilson, W. Stewart Agras, Denise Wilfley, and Marsha Marcus.

During my years at UCLA I have had the good fortune of working closely with the immensely talented professional staff of the Eating Disorders Program of the Lynda & Stewart Resnick Neuropsychiatric Hospital, especially Roberta Freeman, Lynda Nannes, Cynthia Pikus, Mark DeAntonio, Carlyn Lampert, Cheryl Teplinsky, Mary Johnston, Donnie Hillis, Stacy Bower, Paul Bolita, Jack Kautzer, Elizabeth Froes, Eileen Lubieniecka, Joann Noonan, Nahid Massoud, Grace Kothounian, Elizabeth Simmonds, Shawn Legg, Owen Peterson, Leah Pressman, Redden Crisp, and Rhonda Sena. I have also learned much about what being a parent means from my two children, Nicole and Meredith. Thanks also to those families who were kind enough to share their stories with us in order to make the book come alive.

A great debt is owed to my coauthor, Meg Schneider, for the trust she bestowed in me to work with her on this book, for being patient with my many hesitations and questions about how to best approach the task, and for the energy and enthusiasm she brought to the effort. I am also grateful to Carol Mann for the "push" that ultimately brought me to this project, and to Marnie Cochrane at Da Capo Press, and to Carol Bifulco, for all of the hard work in bringing the book to its completion.

Finally, I stumble for words that can express deeply enough the debt to my wife and best friend, Courtney Marlowe. There is no gift in life more precious than knowing that I will wake every day to her boundless joy and laughter, and that mischievous wink. Thank you, Courtney, for your love and your wisdom.

Michael Strober

In my effort to make sure this book put forth the views of different disciplines and the valuable services of professionals, I asked a lot of questions of a lot of people. They were all generous, informative, and encouraging. Thank you to the following for contributing so much to this project: Jennifer Medina, MS RD, CDE; Lisa Mandelbaum-Brown, MS RD, CDN; Nicole Dilorenzo, RD CDE; Judith Ebenstein, PhD; Karen Salzarulo, LCSW, BCD; Jennifer Torio-Hurley, MSW; Ellie Seidel; Layne Prosperi; Amy Pizer, PhD; and Dana Michie, MSED, LMFT. I would also like to thank those brave, honest, and open families who allowed us to interview them about so many personal things so that we could make these pages as helpful as possible. You know who you are. Then there are my friends and colleagues who were and are relentless cheerleaders: Carol Coleman, Lynn Sonberg, Sandra Edelman, Roger Cooper, and my editor Marnie Cocheran, who manifested such wonderful respect for the project through her sensitive editing. Most special thanks goes to my talented clinical supervisor and friend Bonnie Jacobson, PhD, who always stirs my mind, and to my terrific and smart agent Carol Mann, who seems uniquely equipped to put up with me. My coauthor, Michael Strober, PhD, was such an incredible resource and invaluable partner on this journey. Finally, there are some thank-yous to those who are closest. Thanks to my son Jason, who had to put up with too many "Not now, honey, I'm working" remarks and yet still managed to never get into trouble (well, serious trouble), and to Richard Stone, who consistently makes me feel like I can do anything, while at the same time always saving me from my worst self.

Meg Schneider

one

"I Need to Be Thinner"

Jennifer turned from right to left in front of the mirror peering intently at what seemed to be a . . . a . . . gentle hill of a stomach. She frowned and glanced at the magazine lying on her bed. The cover featured a bikini-clad model surrounded by the one thing Jennifer was beginning to crave. Boyfriends. Admiring boyfriends. She turned her attention back to the mirror. From the front she looked okay. But, of course, what did that mean? She couldn't stand face-forward in front of every guy all the time.

Nope. It was time to diet. Time for Jennifer to be all that she could be, which to Jennifer meant weighing a lot less than the number flashing on her scale.

Approximately 65 percent of all adolescent girls are thinking along the same lines as Jennifer, even if they don't all have boyfriends in mind. They may be seeking the admiration of their peers in general or reaching for a look they've come to believe is the only truly acceptable one. Perhaps it's the media, messages picked up at home, teasing remarks, low self-esteem, the beginning of a depression, anxiety, or an expression of a deep obsessive need to be perfect. It almost doesn't matter at this moment.

What matters is that Jennifer wants to diet because she thinks it's the only way to be or get what she wants. Dieting is a salvation, the road to pure happiness, or at least a means of becoming popular. And as time goes by, if need be she may find it the seemingly perfect weapon to slay the demons of insecurity, helplessness, imperfection, and fear.

Dieting, she may come to believe, is her ticket to a better life.

She will not, however, say this, which looms as a problem.

Jennifer will appear to most others as perfectly normal. Perhaps, by most standards, she even is. So she wants to lose a little weight. True, it hardly seems necessary, but what harm can it do? At the dinner table, Jennifer might comment that she'd like to lose a few pounds, and her parents smile and shrug it off. What teenage girl doesn't want to lose weight, they might think?

Well, they're right.

And what's there to worry about, they might also think? Look at her. A good student, a fine athlete, well organized, occasionally moody but essentially a very social and involved child. This dieting is hardly something that necessitates attention.

But what if they're wrong?

The moment your daughter begins to comment about her weight may, in fact, be the best time to sit up and take notice. It doesn't mean that you should DO something immediately. Not at all. In fact, to say or do anything this early in the game could actually deepen whatever anxieties are playing into your child's plan, which in turn could shorten her path to an eating disorder. But this *does* mean that you ought to start watching for the moment when and if an appropriate "understanding dialogue" should begin. We will address what that means and what such an exchange might look like later on in this book.

Suffice it to say that some diets are just that—a brief episode of calorie, fat, or carb counting. They are merely attempts to lose weight for the sake of a one-size-smaller skirt. Others, however, are a prelude to the kind of problem with food that has nothing to do with shape or size but rather emotional issues, which left undetected could bring your child to the brink of seriously disordered eating behavior. And one kind can become the other quickly and quietly. You need to know the difference and be vigilant for a change in behavior that might be signaling the change from one kind of diet to another. This book is your guide to that understanding and detection.

The number of adolescents exhibiting disturbing behaviors is staggering:

Among teens of normal weight, 40–60 percent see themselves as too heavy.

Up to 60 percent of all teens diet regularly.

More than 50 percent of teens exercise to improve their shape or weight.

Approximately 45 percent smoke cigarettes as a form of weight control.

The large majority of teens are preoccupied with their food intake.

Approximately 70 percent of girls feel that shape is important for their self-esteem and thus fear gaining weight.

Body dissatisfaction is quite common in teens, the majority of whom tend to overestimate the actual size of their body parts, thus making them feel generally larger than they truly are.

So, with all of this body-conscious behavior going on, how can you recognize when a desire to be thin is mutating into a struggle to feel good, and if it does, what can you do to prevent your child from developing a disorder that at best would compromise his or her health, psychological well-being, and cognitive abilities and at worst mean a lifelong struggle to maintain a healthy weight and avoid hospitalization?

This is a book about helping your child either steer clear of or maneuver herself off a slippery slope that could lead to an eating disorder known as anorexia nervosa. It's about what you as a parent can do and say to help your child feel good about herself, keep her body image intact, and cope with all the outside influences and emotional issues in her life. It's a book that will help you understand and support your child whether or not she is dieting intensively and no matter where she rests on the continuum of eating disordered behaviors.

This is *not* a book about anorexia nervosa. It's about teens whom we will refer to in this book as having a problem with food (or dieting), flirting with an eating disorder, being excessive dieters, or having eating disordered behaviors. The difference between "on the brink" and anorexia nervosa is an important one. Understanding the facts will help you become aware of the subtle road to an eating disorder and at the same time see the difference between a problem and pathology—a distinction that will impact on the tenor of the interventions that are necessary.

DEFINING THE TRUE PATHOLOGY

Anorexia nervosa is a frightening and puzzling eating disorder, most basically characterized by an intense fear of gaining weight, a marked distortion of body shape and size, and an inability to maintain a minimally normal body weight (quantified as being less than 85 percent of what would be expected; see the BMI charts in the appendix for specifics). Adolescents who suffer with anorexia nervosa fear the conflicts that come about with puberty, have very limited emotional expression, and often have marked perfectionism and self-doubt. They are generally malnourished and face serious medical complications as their weight loss progresses. Occasionally, people with anorexia nervosa will try purging as an additional way to lose weight. They may also occasionally binge in reaction to intense hunger or in the process of restoring a normal weight. (This should not be confused with bulimia nervosa.) Oddly enough, their intense fear of fat is not alleviated by any amount of weight loss. Even the threat of death is not enough to dissuade them from their dangerous course. Fortunately, anorexia nervosa affects only 0.1 to 0.3 percent of females in the general population and even fewer males.

Bulimia nervosa—or simply bulimia as it is known outside of medical circles—fits into the picture a little differently than anorexia. Dieting can persist for quite a while before it brings a child to a diagnosable state of anorexia nervosa. However, with the characteristic repeated cycles of regular binge eating and purging, bulimia can be diagnosed within a few months of onset of the behavior. With bulimia, binge activity may also be compensated for by misuse of laxatives, diuretics, or enemas or appetite-reducing drugs. As with anorexia nervosa, people suffering from bulimia have a distorted view of their bodies, but their problem can often go unnoticed since people with the binge eating disorder maintain a near normal weight, even though repeated vomiting can seriously compromise their health. In other words, there is hardly a slippery slope with bulimia. It is quickly an illness, and a well-kept secret illness at that. Bulimia is not the focus of this book, as the path to the disorder cannot be tracked or managed in the same way as the road to anorexia nervosa.

Bulimia and anorexia nervosa are unmistakably serious disorders for which adolescents need swift and consistent medical and psychological intervention. But again, they affect only a minority of teens in the general population. In other words, a progression from problem dieting to clinically severe eating is the exception, not the rule. Still, however, some adolescents can come dangerously close, and problem dieting has its own serious issues, even if those issues are not always life-threatening. They may not step over the line where dieting and fear of food take on a life of their own in an all-consuming fight for body control, but these dieters can, as they move closer to a diagnosable illness, run the risk of difficult and potentially damaging physical problems.

The group of preadolescents and adolescents we are concerned with in this book comprises a significant population that is fast on the rise. This is the company upon whose door Jennifer has come knocking. And, truthfully, the odds are that she'll be welcomed by the crowd, happy to include her into the fold. "Getting thin" can be, as we will explain a bit later, used as a kind of currency, unfortunately replacing others such as shared interests.

THE SLIPPERY SLOPE

Girls who are dieting strenuously can be placed along a three-stage continuum that we refer to as the *slippery slope* and that leads to poor health, even if not a diagnosed eating disorder. It is important for you as a concerned parent to note, however, that this slope has exits. No matter what stage she is in or whether she is at the beginning, middle, or end of that stage's parameters, she can get off and, with your help, return to firm and healthy ground. Even if she is at the brink.

At the brink, these preadolescents and adolescents are often clinically referred to as having "subclinical" disturbance or as "Eating Disordered NOS" (not otherwise specified). Their symptoms and distress don't reach the level associated with full-blown eating disorders but could progress if they are allowed to travel through the stages that mark the prepathology period.

These girls, the ones on the brink, are plagued by uncontrollably obsessive thoughts about weight and engage excessively in methods to control it. They're dieting and exercising overzealously, possibly experimenting with purging (vomiting) or using laxatives after a particularly hearty meal. And as a further hint at the emergence of unnatural preoccupations, they may be critical of others for ignoring the importance of good nutrition or even incredulous that they themselves are not widely admired for the "purity" of their eating and exercising behavior. Occasionally they may lapse into a chaotic pattern of binge eating, lending the false impression that the dieting is over. Usually it is not.

Here is the way in which we are defining, or delineating, these three stages.

Stage One: The Innocent (but Rigid) Dieter

She's thinking that it's time to get thin. She needs to lose a few pounds. She selects a diet and sticks to it. Every day she checks to see what's happened. She introduces exercise into her daily routine. What, she asks if questioned, could be healthier than the way she is now treating her body? The pounds begin to come off, but to the casual eye she is still looking good, if not a bit too slender.

Stage Two: The Exhilarated Dieter

Success. She's receiving lots of compliments. Maybe, she thinks, she can do better. Now she's studying calorie and carbohydrate charts. She is preoccupied a good deal of the day with decisions about what to eat. She can't wait to exercise off what she's just eaten. The pounds are slowly coming off. She feels powerful. A little hungry, too, but she can master that.

Stage Three: The Obsessed and Preoccupied Dieter

Immediately upon waking, and then throughout the day, she is planning what she will and will not eat and precisely when. She's strategizing how she can keep it to herself, since most people don't seem to understand how important this is. She wonders if she can squeeze in two hours at the track. What she sees in the mirror—fifteen pounds lighter than her starting goal of a five-pound loss—still doesn't seem right. Not her thighs, anyway. She's been feeling a bit tired lately, but it can't be the food thing because she hardly feels hungry. Just a little. She's wishing people would just leave her alone.

Let her "eat" in her room. Everything would be great. Also, the smells in the kitchen are kind of nauseating—when they're not filling her with uncontrollable desire and cravings. This girl is on the brink.

Over time one stage can seamlessly melt into another almost before anything is noticed, which is why parents are confused. Children nursing eating disorders are actually masters at putting up smoke screens and tossing out excuses—faking to the right then moving to the left, as it were. Specifically, the signs of being on the brink of an eating disorder might look (and be excused by the adolescent herself) like this:

- Body dissatisfaction particularly in girls who mature early ("I can't stand my hips. No one else has them! I will change this no matter what!")
- Skipping meals ("Sorry, I had a big snack at school.")
- Fasting for twenty-four hours ("It's just to cleanse my system.")
- Weight loss to the very bottom of normal for an adolescent of a particular build and height. Slowly the weight drops into slightly below normal without worry or fear of healthy consequences ("I'm fine. I feel great!")
- Excessive exercising ("I have to stay in shape for volleyball," something the coach would agree with.)
- Preferring to eat in private ("I have a lot of homework to do.")
- A tendency toward perfectionism in everything she does ("I can't believe the teacher gave me an A–.")
- Developing odd eating habits such as cutting things into tiny pieces ("It's fun eating like this. Besides, I won't choke.")
- When eating, picks only low-fat foods or decides on vegetarianism ("I hate carcinogens.")
- Vomiting after an occasional big meal ("Something must have been spoiled," she might say if she is caught.)
- Sudden episodes of bingeing ("See! I'm eating!")

- Doesn't seem to be hungry in regular cycles, often overeating or undereating. She may seem to binge (eat a pint of ice cream) and then try to starve the next day.
- Studying food labels for fat and carb content and every few days or so grumbling about why everything good has to be so fattening ("I'm becoming health-conscious!")
- May feel uncomfortable both emotionally and physically after eating due to anxiety over the caloric intake, as if one meal could catapult her into a size 18 ("I'm not irritable, I just haven't been sleeping a lot.")
- Begins to consider various diet plans and rigidly applies herself. Certainly, and unfortunately, they are easy to find. Atkins, South Beach, Weight Watchers, and Jenny Craig assail our senses every day with their promises of a beautiful body ("Sorry that's not allowed on my diet.")

Some girls will have almost all, some, or only a few of the above symptoms, but suffice it to say that the deeper her fears about eating are allowed to grow, the faster she will plummet into a hole from which she will find it harder and harder to escape. This is because not eating weakens her emotionally, cognitively, and physically. Her ideas about food and eating will become increasingly distorted, and the feelings of inadequacy, anger, or depression will intensify, although her access to her emotions will lessen as the obsession with food grows.

THE BODY CANVAS

As dieting slips into irrational degrees of food restrictions, the body becomes the canvas upon which a girl illustrates her emotional troubles. As one 15-year-old girl said when asked what she feels like when she looks in the mirror, "Usually I think I look good. But if I've had a bad day everything looks bad. Thighs, butt, even my

ankles." In truth this is a benign enough statement. None of us feel
we look great when we aren't feeling happy with ourselves. But one
has to notice that she doesn't say, "But if I've had a day in which I
feel stupid and ignored by everyone." If she could recognize *those*
issues as the root of her problems that day, would she then still focus
the hurt on her body?

Girls can frequently begin to lose their voice in favor of a physical expression of unhappiness. They only vaguely realize that they
are using body talk instead of using emotional talk. And as success
slowly builds and their bodies appear to be more and more under
control, they begin to feel comforted. But it can become a comfort
that never feels good enough—and thus one more pound slips off,
and then another, and ironically all the while unhappiness, emotional disorientation, and confusion grow. These girls aren't managing their internal world. They are instead closing down shop. And
the question, beyond wanting to be thin, is why?

She may have poor self-esteem and believe that by attaining a
particular weight she will finally like herself and others will admire
her. She may be depressed and unable to find the words to define
how she is feeling.

She may also have a strong adversity to conflict. She may have
a tendency to turn unhappiness inward so that she allows her body
to express the deprivation she feels psychologically and emotionally.
Feeling unable to control those things that are making her unhappy,
or even to understand them, she may seek comfort by controlling
the one thing that totally belongs to her. Her body. It may start with
"I'll feel better if I'm thinner" but end up on a slippery slope to an
eating disorder as she tries harder and harder to feel okay.

Penelope may have a tendency toward obsessive and perfectionist
thinking. Is my homework done exactly right? Are my clothes folded
correctly? Is my hair perfectly combed? In order to feel pretty, everything about me has to be perfect. This obsessive thinking can easily
find its way into the quest for a perfect body—a constant counting of

Penelope, age 13, had tried and tried, but a straight-A report card wasn't going to happen. Her father had harped and harped about it, and finally one evening upon receiving her grades averaging B+ he simply announced, "I give up," walking with disgust out of the room.

Later that evening Penelope went through her usual presleep routine of studying her naked body in the mirror. It had seemed okay before. She looked good in clothes, anyway. Most of the time. Penelope looked a little closer this particular time at her thighs. They seemed larger. Fuller. Ever since her period.

Penelope shook her head. "Nope. I'm not letting that happen," she whispered out loud. The next morning she skipped breakfast and that afternoon had a green salad for lunch. She wasn't "giving up" until her thighs looked like the girl on the cover of Teen Vogue.

calories and fat grams and pretty soon meeting daily with a scale to make sure everything is just so, and falling. This is particularly true for teens whose personality is marked by an enormous capacity for discipline focus and compulsiveness, as these same traits will be factors in her efforts to restrict food and lose weight. In other words, the diet of such a teen will be more rigid, more compulsive, and thus more successful as well as potentially more overzealous compared to the teen who lacks these personality traits.

Since most problem dieting and eating disorders begin around puberty, it is fair to say that there is a very large developmental component to the "whys" of control. A teenager's body is changing, necessarily shifting and gaining curves and weight. Social expectations are rising. Hormones are accelerated, and the way in which the body is changing is now taking on tremendous importance. Sexual attraction is becoming a preoccupation. Puberty comes with greater expectations of independent thought, increasing sexual impulses, and formation of social bonds away from the family. It is the harbinger of adulthood and all that implies biologically, socially, and psychologically. Adolescents, especially those with pressures coming from other arenas, can feel out of control—almost panicked—though this experience is masked by increasing interest in dieting and weight loss. Ironically it's an escape, but an escape to a far more dangerous place.

WHAT ABOUT BOYS?

By and large, the research evidence suggests that eating disorders in males resemble those experienced by females. Twenty years ago it was thought that for every ten to fifteen women with anorexia or bulimia there was one man with these disorders. Today there are relatively few studies of boys, and those that exist point more to an interest in developing muscle than "getting thin." Boys tend to be more concerned about developing a "six pack" than actually attaining skinniness, which they see as feminine, but they are falling prey in increasing numbers to the images on TV and in magazines. An anonymous, informal survey we conducted with boys revealed a concern about looking "strong." The sentence fragment "If I had the perfect body" was completed with such statements as "I'd be strong and muscular," "I'd get all the girls," and perhaps most poignantly "people might actually look at me." Clearly, whereas females become weight-preoccupied and desire thinness as puberty arrives, males desire musculature. On the whole, boys seem to want to "bulk up." Yet even despite this, for the most part as compared to girls, boys who were asked what they think when they look in the mirror do not have nearly as critical an internal dialogue as girls.

Throughout this book we will make reference to the female gender for the sake of consistency and to respect the significantly larger percentage of problems experienced by female adolescents. However, much of the advice and information will apply to adolescent boys as well.

OTHER TRIGGERS FOR A FEAR OF GAINING WEIGHT

Not all overly enthusiastic dieters are burdened with serious emotional problems. Still, it's fairly certain that there are other issues that play into this quest for the body ideal. These issues may not worsen with time, but they still need attention in order for your child to live comfortably in her own shoes.

The Sports Piece

Sports by their very nature create an arena in which the body becomes a central focus of critical inspection. Many of the females showcased in sports are figure skaters, gymnasts, and tennis players. Their outfits count. The question then becomes for girls, am I supposed to look good or play well? Well-meaning coaches anxious for a tip-top team will also hold to certain weight requirements, unknowingly pressuring young athletes to lose weight. This issue is particularly a problem for boys and wrestling—a sport in which a particular weight, down to the half pound, can result in sitting out an event. The restrictive dieting that many young men must undertake is often unhealthy and in some cases, once the wrestling season is over, not so easy to put aside. Team sports, then, that are supposed to offer camaraderie can ironically become yet another isolating arena.

The Genetic Piece

Research indicates that eating disorders have a genetic component that requires an environmental factor to express itself. The trigger for genetically at-risk women could be the emphasis society places on lean bodies. Possible traits that increase risk for eating disorders

include metabolic factors that allow for rapid weight loss when calorie intake is restricted, previously mentioned personality traits that
allow for more compulsive dieting behavior, a predisposition to
excessive anxiety, and low self-esteem. These issues will be covered
in more detail in chapter 10.

Messages at Home

The home environment can play a significant role in a child's flirtation with an eating disorder. Does the adolescent feel as if he or she
has no say in decisions made at home? Do parents talk about their
own weight and the merits of a slender body? Is much expected of
this child that is hard to fulfill? Is the atmosphere in the home one
that discourages conflict and expressions of anger? Is there an
emphasis on rules and accomplishments? Is a child's weaknesses
noted more often than her strengths? Is the child having difficulty
separating from the parent, leaving the child frustrated by the
dependence and anxious to break free of the ties she feels? All of
these issues can play a part in the development of the kinds of emotional problems that can set the stage for eating disorders.

The Cultural Piece

It hardly needs to be said that we live in a body-conscious society.
Pressure to be thin from one's social environment encourages body
dissatisfaction, and repeated messages that one cannot be thin
enough can produce discontent with physical appearance. The
media is particularly powerful, and its effect appears to be gaining
strength. Many professionals believe that the rates of anorexia nervosa have indeed steadily increased since 1950.

A recent radio ad for a shoe company had one teenager asking the
other if she could borrow her brand new shoes for a date. The
response understandably was a resounding "NO! I haven't even worn
them yet myself." "Well," the first teenager replied, "if you let me bor-

row them I'll let you wear those jeans of mine you like—the ones that make your thighs look SO thin." Bingo. The shoes changed hands.

The message? *Anything* for a skinny pair of thighs.

And what of the recent spate of makeover shows? Yes, they work on everything from hair to teeth, but almost always there's a liposuction performed on some part of the body. A suck-out-the-fat solution. And in the end it's like a coronation. Finally, she's royalty.

The School Piece

School is a potential hotbed for all manner of problems. Countless girls report that they spend an inordinate amount of time checking each other out. Conversations in the hallways are peppered everyday with such statements as "I feel so fat." Or "Do these jeans make me look fat?" Or "I just got my period and my stomach is out to HERE!" Instantly come the replies. "You don't look fat. Stop it!" "No, you look great!" "Yeah. I hate when that happens." The truth is that most of the time neither the questions nor the answers are the true topics being discussed.

What's really being said is, "I don't feel good today." "Am I okay?" "I'm not sure I want to grow up." And the answers have become the language of friendship—the unfortunate place girls go to express solidarity. "You look so thin! Don't worry!" Yes, sometimes you'll hear "I think I failed that test" followed by a quick "I'm sure you didn't." But for the most part girls in middle school and high school report that conversations surrounding weight always seem to rule the day—and for the most part each girl privately knows that somewhere she is really expressing distress about other things.

One girl explains, "*When I say I'm feeling fat, I'm really saying I feel terrible. It kind of all gets mixed up in my head. So when someone replies, 'Oh, no you don't,' I know I'm supposed to feel better, but I don't. I just didn't know what to say to begin with, and then I really don't know what to say after. So I just mumble 'Oh good' or something when I really mean, 'Yeah? Well I still feel bad.'*"

Many girls report that an added very real pressure comes from boys whom they often view as hypercritical of their weight and general looks. Each day brings a fresh, new effort to look perfect, to avoid being teased, to be sure some boy won't turn around and make a snide remark just loud enough for them to hear, such as "Well, she's approaching an oink." Some girls react to this critical tendency with deep resentment. Others bypass that altogether and go straight to feeling ugly. But almost all of them feel put down and silenced, trapped in a world that can feel like nothing more than a magnifying glass focused entirely on a real or imagined flaw.

School can be experienced as a courtroom, a nonstop hall of judgment. But so is the competitive world in which your children live, and sometimes, if an adolescent is not imbued with a solid sense of self-worth, it can feel as if there is nothing to do or any words to use that could make it okay to just be who you are.

A NOTE ON ETHNICITY

It seems clear that eating disorders are affected by cultural circumstances and values. Anorexia nervosa and bulimia develop predominantly in countries where an abundance of food exists. Famine is a condition that engenders virtually no cases of eating disorders.

But the times hold sway as well. Previous generations in the United States equated larger bodies with prosperity. Now, however, we tend to expect thinness in women of affluence. Much has been said about anorexia being a Caucasian middle- to upper-middle-class illness. But researchers for the most part are suspecting that it is still a question of the values in which we are immersed and that as more and more people of differing ethnicity, including Hispanics and African Americans, become acculturated into our society, increases in eating disorders will follow. It has been postulated, for example, that as African Americans become more affluent and adopt traditional white middle-class values, they are more likely to develop the disorders associated with the white American group. This may account for the slowly growing percentage of African Americans who are showing signs of eating disorders. A generation or so ago, African Americans who did not identify with white values seemed to more easily have rejected thinness, embracing their own concept of feminine beauty. As a group they still seem more accepting of their bodies. But the cultural values issue is critical. Our concept of thinness is indeed spreading across many ethnic lines.

Certainly one also cannot overlook the possibility that as a culture, Caucasian Americans, both the general population and the medical establishment, are more alert to signs of eating disorders than other cultures, which could influence to some degree the seeming ethnic differences.

However, it should be noted that even in middle- to upper-class families, there have been many instances of pediatricians examining a girl who is most definitely on the slippery slope of an eating disorder, noting to parents breezily, for example, "Don't worry about her weight. It's a stage. She still has SOME fat on her."

Our awareness of our values does not necessarily translate into a form of protection. We still can be blinded by a lack of understanding for the emotional lives of our children and how their emotions impact their physical selves.

YOU'LL HEAR A LOT ABOUT "CONTROL"

Lara, a 5'1", fine-boned 12-year-old sat primly in the therapist's office for her first visit. She weighs all of 92 pounds. Her hair was shiny, her eyes bright. A plastic smile was settled on her face. "I'm fine," Lara said. "Everything is good. My mom wants me here to get things off my chest." She clutched a neatly zipped little handbag on her lap.

"What things?" the therapist asked.

"I don't know," Lara replied sweetly, playing with the folds of her skirt and still smiling. The therapist noted that she was quite thin. But other than that she looked well.

After inquiring about her sleeping patterns, homework schedule, and other innocuous topics, the therapist queried, "And your eating habits? Three meals?" Leaning forward conspiratorially, Lara replied with a forced, soft chuckle, "My mother must have told you she thinks I'm getting anorexia. But as you see that's so insane."

"Oh," replied the therapist. "What do I see?"

Swiftly and with a flourish the girl pulled out a spanking new, wrapped chocolate bar from her bulky quilted jacket that she had kept buttoned throughout the session. "SEE!" she announced triumphantly. "I'll be eating this on the way home."

How clever, the therapist thought to herself. Her client had brought a prop.

Lara is a girl on the brink. She's decidedly too thin. She had noted to her therapist that she fainted recently in gym class but dismissed this as due to her impending period. Her mother had an eating disorder too when she was young and, while claiming to be concerned for her daughter, consistently packed salads for her daughter's lunch, sans cheese, eggs, or meat. Lara is, however, still eating some normal meals, and this was convincing her mom that all was okay. She had actually brought Lara because they seemed to be arguing a lot. Lara had been very irritable lately. But Lara didn't agree.

Lara claimed to feel "just fine." Lara, in fact, literally proclaimed, "I am in control."

People often say when speaking about a child with an eating problem that it's all about *control*. This is a vague, confusing concept. After all, isn't this child *out* of control? Isn't her dieting irrational? Isn't she exercising like a person gone mad? Isn't she living in a house of funny mirrors?

The answer to all of these questions is *yes*. But only in accordance with her parent's world. Not hers. To her she is in nothing short of excellent control. It's her body, and she can make it do what she wants. She lives with the idea of mind over body. She is training herself to tolerate hunger, and when she begins to grow thin, her pride starts to build.

But for many of these extreme, obsessively dieting teens, the power to *control* weight is a direct reaction to the aspects of their lives that they feel are beyond their control.

In other words, she is seeking a discipline that becomes increasingly more elusive. The longer the diet continues, the less she will have control, though tragically she perceives just the opposite. She is buried in a travesty, a parody of control. Our job as professionals and yours as parents is to help her gain back the healthy control she has abdicated to her fears. And that is the purpose of this book.

COPING WITH HOW *YOU* FEEL

Eating disorders are frightening. So is the slippery slope that can lead to a serious problem. There can be a long period in which parents are completely unaware that anything is going on. In retrospect, this can be at best disturbing and at worst deeply distressing. Parents may experience everything from guilt ("I know it was something I must have said"), to anger ("Why is she doing this to me?"), to profound depression born of a feeling of helplessness ("I just can't reach her"). In almost all cases parents experience a certain amount of shame—because no matter what, it's happening to their child; it's a problem that few understand; rarely can they find people with whom to share their feelings, and even more rarely do they want to. We've seen many mothers be both seething and heartbroken at the same time over their child's dieting. Something, they think, must be terribly wrong with their daughter, themselves, or the entire family.

Remember: The causes of eating disorders are *multifactorial*. This means that it isn't just about you and your child, though it can easily feel that way. The other factors we've spoken of earlier interact in unpredictable ways with how your adolescent might function in the world.

If you recognize your child on these pages, you have time to pull her back from the brink of an eating disorder. Just remember that her thinness, to her, is her ticket to ride.

Consider yourself her traveling companion. You'll be sitting several seats away, but she'll know you're there. You will both be watching each other out of the corners of your eyes. The key is for her to know that you are aware of her, that you know her and want to understand her, quietly finding ways to be mindful of and change her world, and are ready to give her whatever help she needs.

When this happens, chances are that she will stand up and slowly, perhaps with misgivings (but you can handle that!), join you in the dining car.

two
___

The Media Factor

When 17-year-old Maria Sharapova beat Serena Williams for the women's title at Wimbledon in 2004, a reporter compared her to another good-looking Russian tennis player, Anna Kournikova. Maria commented simply, "I don't pay attention to that at all. I never considered myself as a pin-up. I never will."

If only this were the message our daughters consistently received from every famous young female whose accomplishments are far more important than her appearance. Unfortunately, troubling messages are everywhere. One newspaper commented about Maria Sharapova, "She has legs like a model." Are we to believe that being thin and beautiful is most often the only way to "play ball"? Since you can't edit every magazine you see or monitor every TV program, screening out the message is impossible. But as parents you can learn how to help your adolescent child discriminate between what's real and healthy in the face of media manipulation, hype, and misstatements.

THE CHALLENGE

There's a print ad we've seen countless times in magazines hawking a diet pill. On the left is a picture of a slim young woman wearing a bikini. She looks lovely but very sad. A bit like a beaten dog. On the right is the same woman, only now she's skinny. She's also smiling triumphantly, hands on hips. The line underneath reads, "You too can look like this!!"

So, imagine your adolescent daughter glancing over this ad. Assuming she hasn't yet developed a problem with body image or eating, she will likely look at the picture on the left and think, "Hmm. I wouldn't mind looking like that." Then she'll look at the picture on the right. There will likely be a moment of confusion—a kind of reshuffling of the mental cards in order to make sense of this new information. Here is what she'll come away with:

- Slim is okay. Skinny is better.
- The skinnier you are, the happier you are.
- Everyone's body is built just like the body in the picture—if only one diets correctly.
- And finally, and perhaps most importantly, of course you want to look like the girl on the right! Who wouldn't?

Our children, and most especially our girls, are being raised in a culture in which it seems that appearance is the most tradable commodity in their possession. Yes, it's good to be smart, and sparkly and trustworthy and empathic. But first, you need to look good.

And good means thin.

This message is carried to us in magazines and on television, radio, and silver screens everywhere. Visually we are saturated, literally bombarded with images of the "perfect" body. Any adolescent whose body is in the process of developing into that of a woman will quickly focus intently on these images. Will that be me, she might ask herself, dreading the horrifying risk of not being thin enough?

She'll spot the "How to Lose 5 Pounds in One Week" magazine article in the blink of an eye, hoping against hope that it's the magic bullet. This is because these girls/women with the beautiful, tight, thin bodies seem to have the most fun, get the most guys, and enjoy an abundance of confidence. The implication is that the girls with a bit too much weight or less than perfect bodies struggle through life, too often left out, not having dates or the right guy, and feeling timid around others.

You might ask how a wonderfully bright young adolescent could buy into this idea that slimness and beauty are everything. Aren't young women increasingly striving for interesting careers, valuing their brains, striving for success? The answer, of course, is yes. But one does not necessarily negate the other.

There are, we believe, four main reasons for this:

1. In spite of the pervasive influence of the media, adolescents bring their own belief systems and sensitivities to media messages. They could just as easily concentrate on the articles and ads that stress our individuality. How intently they buy into the media's prescription for improved appearance and importance of striving for physical perfection will have a lot to do with their own sense of selfworth. This is not to say that a confident girl can't fall prey to our culture's insistence that thin is best. But remember that confidence in one aspect of life doesn't necessarily generalize to all other aspects of functioning. Then, too, a depressed adolescent may not pay the media much mind at all. Perhaps issues of diet and weight are not the "place" she goes when feeling down. She may instead obsess about the size of her nose or brood because she has not yet learned how to manage her shyness. Rather than diet, she stays home and reads, hiding but eating normally. Still, it's safe to say that the more vulnerable an adolescent is—the more inferior or lonely or even angry she feels—the chances begin to increase that the media and its message will start to feel like a solution worth trying.

2. The message that one needs to "fit the mold" is so pervasive, in so many magazines, in so many TV programs and movies, that the

body beautiful has become *normalized*. Lovely, slim bodies are ever present. If you don't have one, it's hard not to think of yourself as unusual. And as any teen will tell you, being different is not exactly a goal. Teenagers are, at this time, almost to a one trying to "fit in." Can you imagine the fear experienced by a girl who looks in the mirror and realizes that if the camera were focused on her she'd likely be featured on the "Disaster" pages in a fashion magazine where a big black slash covers the face of the perpetrator of imperfection? Of course these articles address reality, but always in a corrective mode. Magazines everywhere talk about how to make short legs look longer, and fat thighs look thinner, and thick waists appear narrower, and heavy arms seem slimmer. You never see the headline "What's So Bad About Round Hips?" or "Short Legs Can Be Beautiful Too."

3. Our culture and media have failed, in a consistent way, to point out the myth that a thin (and thus gorgeous) body is all you need to achieve happiness. As adults we know that having a great shape is hardly a ticket to success. We glance at the enviable images before us and think, "I'd have loved to look like that," but then most adults are able to go about our lives filled with affirmations of other sorts, feeling happy and fulfilled. When we get dressed up we are fine with looking really good by *our* standards. But our daughters haven't had our life experiences. They are living in a world of affirmations of beauty. Their accomplishments at this point are necessarily limited, as is their sense of personal power and self-regard. If they aren't slim, then what are they? We forget this. We assume that our smart daughters will take pride in their brains and make peace with their thighs. But maybe they can't. Or at least not without our help.

As one girl said, *"I'm so envious when I look at those pictures. Their bodies look insane. I know they aren't real, but then I think I'd still want to look like that. It doesn't make sense I know. But it hurts to think there are all those gorgeous people out there and I didn't get the luck."*

4. The media objectifies the body, making it something to admire apart from the person inside. What a distorted perspective! Instead of an integrated whole, the more girls try to *work on* individual

aspects of their outside selves, the more they fail to see themselves as composites of emotional, intellectual, and physical characteristics. They can no longer say, "Basically I'm pretty cool," because they cannot tear their eyes away from the offending detail. The body is something to assess, to judge, to pick on. It is something to hate or see as the enemy. Photographs that chop the body into pieces to be analyzed separately, showing thick thighs or a slim waist or a round backside encourage readers to see the parts instead of the whole. The concept of looking in the mirror and seeing a *person* gets lost. In fact, and although it's a strong statement, in our society it has almost become a social offense to see oneself as acceptable physically.

IF WE FEEL OKAY, THAT'S NOT OKAY

There was, early on in a popular TV series, a scene in which four grown women were considering a fashion magazine. The dialogue started in a very politically correct way. There were complaints about the beautiful models and the impossibility of looking like that. One woman expresses how distressed she feels about her own thighs when glancing over the pictures. Two of her friends immediately insist that she is being ridiculous. Then after a pause, one wishes for a better chin and another a different nose. All the while the fourth woman is quiet.

The first woman looks at her silent friend expectantly. It is clear what she is waiting for. It's Ms. Silent's turn to offer up her own personal insecurity in this moment of shared imperfection. It is as if there *has* to be something, and if there isn't, well, who does she think she is?

Finally comes a wonderful moment, but unfortunately it is given short shrift. The fourth woman at the table simply refuses to offer anything up. The others gasp, but she holds firm. "I like the way I look!" she exclaims with not a shred of apology in her voice.

After a brief pause, they all laugh. The message was, isn't that just like her? Always feeling good about herself. How funny.

But it isn't funny. It's grand.

What this shows is that we are expected to not like something about the way we look. It's supposed to be specific. In admitting to not liking something about ourselves, we are joining the crowd, we are being social.

Similarly, *Mean Girls*, a recent popular film about teenage cliques, included a scene in which three girls voice—in an almost ritualistic fashion—a complaint about their physical selves. One girl stretches so far as to select her nail beds as a source of distress. Although *Mean Girls* could be viewed as a parody of this teenage behavior, it's still true that more and more adolescents are getting the message that of course there must be something not quite good enough about their physical selves, and if they dare to think otherwise then clearly they're blind, insensitive, conceited, or even antisocial.

It's important to select *something* to bemoan. It is, it seems, though of course this is never said, the only polite thing to do.

THE TRUTH HURTS

Remember the girl above who said that she just didn't get the luck of looking like a model? Many girls *do* feel shortchanged. And we *do* have to acknowledge that while what they are looking at is doctored, many of the models and actors are beautiful and born with enviable bodies. In fact, so are some "regular" people.

Don't be afraid to put it out there—to affirm some feelings your daughter has. "Yes. I used to wish I looked like Susan Sarandon. I still do," you might say. "But I feel good about the way I look. It's me." It's critical that you recognize your child's disappointment or envy. In fact, as you read this book you will see that to face the facts of your daughter's world is an important component of building a trusting relationship with her. Your daughter will hear nothing if you do not affirm the realities of her world as she sees them or if you fail to admit that in fact looks and weight can be important.

The trick is to balance this recognition with the idea that there is still room for self-satisfaction and pleasure in being the best that you can be.

This is a very important concept.

Many girls report being driven half mad by their tendency to see themselves in comparison to others, whether it be a movie star or real-life person.

"I just can't stop. I'm always looking to see if I look better than someone else. Even my own friends! I'm comparing in my head our hair, our makeup, the size of our chests. It's sick. I hate it. But a good friend just told me she does the same thing, too."

It is important to remind your daughter that there will always be those who would seem to have more than we do and to acknowledge that there are many who would look at what she has and envy her. At the same time, sympathizing with her disappointment is equally important. "It must be great to feel like the whole world thinks you're beautiful," you might say. Then remind her that she is a person with her own unique set of qualities. Some are lovely on the outside, some lovely on the inside. If she can appreciate herself more, others will too. She may not instantly buy it. But she'll remember you said it. And with a little luck she'll draw on the thought when she needs it most.

Now let's take a closer look at what our adolescents are specifically up against, and what you as a parent can do about it.

ADVERTISEMENTS

Stories in magazines carry much the same message as the advertisers appearing on their pages. But advertisements tend to be more extreme and thus can appeal to the most insecure audience, who feel themselves most in need of "help."

No matter what the product, the promise is the ease of acquiring beauty. If you use this shampoo, your hair will cascade over your shoulders like a lustrous waterfall. If you try this mascara, your eyelashes will thicken and curl and become a focal point of your face. This lip gloss will give your mouth the perfect shape, and a particular kind of exercise machine will give you the body you've always wanted.

The problem, of course, is that we all want whatever we define as the ideal, and we desire it quickly. Advertisements tell us what that "ideal" is, and so we seek to transform ourselves. But advertisements conveniently neglect one critical fact: Most of us are not physically able to look like the person on TV or in the magazines, and in fact that person doesn't necessarily look that way either. The hair is likely enhanced by extensions or computer; the lashes are probably fake; the lip gloss only offers shine, not shape; and the body you've always wanted may be one that your genetic makeup prevents you from having.

Advertisements only seem able to define beauty in one way.

There is nothing wrong with striving to be the best we can be, as long as it's about ourselves and isn't distorted by false promises. But the self for many adolescents is not good enough. According to magazines, the list of "pieces" of us that can be made perfect include brows, lips, skin, butt, feet, hips, thighs, stomach, hair, and more. One ad for beautiful nails even featured "Beyond Perfect!" Do we ever pause to consider how bizarre this statement really is?

A single-page advertisement in a teen magazine pictures the beautiful face of an up-and-coming model. Along the top is the headline "Beauty—Finding Your Inner Supermodel."

What does that mean? Are we going to find her inside and pull her out? Does it mean that we're beautiful inside? And *are* supermodels beautiful inside? The sentence makes no clear sense. But then that is likely the point. One can read into it whatever one wants. One reader may think, "If I read this magazine, I can find the supermodel in me and look gorgeous." Another girl who judges herself not so attractive might think, "Well, this will work for other people but not me. I'm a lost cause. I'm the freak." It won't occur to her that most everyone is going to have trouble finding her very own supermodel just waiting to emerge into the light.

And so the struggle begins.

What You Can Do

- First, set the record straight in simple terms. Advertising is about money and exploitation. It preys on our vulnerabilities. There's every reason to explain to an adolescent that they may be getting taken. They hate being tricked. Explain how it works:
  1. Researchers conduct focus groups with teens during which time they try to figure out what teens wish for the most. You want it? They'll make it. Sort of.
  2. Armed with this information they create a product that adolescents will be drawn to, as it promises exactly what they were looking for. Why wouldn't it? These adolescents have already revealed what they want.
  3. Advertising's sole purpose is to get people to buy things. They want your money. They don't really care about correcting your flaws. Nor do they care that what they promise is unrealistic.
- Attempt to ground your adolescent. While watching ads on TV or glancing through magazines, voice your doubts. "Those eyelashes are glued on." "Do you realize most of these photographs aren't entirely real? In fact, they can take inches off a model's body using computers." Make it clear that a lot of what your adolescent is looking at is fake.
- Convey the idea that results are something less than what the ad promises. For example, if your daughter sees an ad for shampoo that promises a lustrous mane but her own hair is very fine and thin, reset her expectations. "You have a different hair type. It's very lovely and soft but it's not like what you're looking at."

- Feel free to express your disgust over advertisements you find offensive. The ad described in chapter 1, in which a girl trades shoes she's never worn for her friend's jeans that make her thighs look thin, is a good example. You might comment, "How absurd. She hasn't worn her new shoes yet herself!" Or "Thin thighs are *that* important? Regular thighs are fine too! Bad trade."

- Finally, play a game of "if the tables were turned." "If I tore out an ad from the paper promising a product that could erase every line on my face and said, 'I have to have this,' what would you think?" Your daughter will likely say something like, "Get a life." Or perhaps more kindly, "Mom, how is that possible?" Then explain that that's exactly how you feel when she looks at ads that promise her things. Rest assured this will give her pause.

MAGAZINES

Teen magazines are notorious for conveying the suggestion that all girls should really only look one way. Certainly more and more they are watching their language (there are increasing articles on looking "cool" rather than looking "thin," and "how to be perfect" articles are giving way to "be the best you can be"). But the cool girls are *still* thin, and the best you can be always involves slimming down.

Here is a sampling of articles that walk a fine line, if not cross it:

"How to Wear a Mini"

This piece showed four girls all with long, slender legs sporting very short miniskirts. Each model looked great. But how many girls have legs like that? What are impressionable readers supposed to think when confronted with this article? All they can know is that here is a crucial fashion trend that looks like garbage on them. One has to ask why they also couldn't show six girls, half with shorter, slightly heavier legs and how they might wear a miniskirt (or a satisfying approximation).

"Role Model: Who Doesn't Want to Look Like Kirsten Dunst?"

This is a little piece on how Kursten Dunst achieves her fresh-faced look, but the title goes beyond that information. It says to the reader, "Come on. Admit it! You wish you looked like her!" The obvious problem is that only her identical twin could do that. Is it not conceivable that some girls wouldn't even care to look like her?! But if you say to girls that this is the ideal, where does that leave them? It's almost a taunt, because the ultimate message is, "Here's what you want—but, sorry." And what of the girl who *doesn't* want Dunst's look? Does that make her odd? Different? Then what?

"Get Your Best Butt: Beach Booty Camp"

This is a brief piece on exercises for toning a backside that features a celebrity fitness guru. She is clad in modest sport clothes and takes the reader through six exercises. The fact that the title says "Your" and not "the" is a step in the right direction, but the instructor has a very slender, muscled body that looks just great already! Also, the mention of her being a celebrity guru implies that if all those beautiful stars turned out so great, maybe we can too. This is a recipe for failure.

In direct contrast to this is an online magazine for girls called *Girl Zone* that stresses the interests, needs, and feelings of REAL girls—part of its mission is to also debunk the mythologies that are put forth in the other magazines. While most swimsuit articles have such titles as "How to Look Great in a Two-Piece Bathing Suit" or "Hot on the Beach," *Girl Zone* featured an article entitled "Every BODY Deserves a Swimsuit." This is an extremely positive message.

So many girls suffer when anticipating a trip to the beach. One survey revealed that most girls who worry about their weight begin obsessing about swimming spots as soon as spring arrives and admit to inventing a million and one excuses for avoiding the sand and sun in the sweltering heat of summer.

Certainly the popular newsstand magazines have their share of articles that speak to eating healthfully and fashion pointers that a girl of any shape can relate to, but for the most part readers will not see themselves on these pages. It is another world, another reality they enter, when flipping the pages. It is constructed to look as if the magazine is *just for you*, but it's really for the *ideal you* as ordained by the culture—and the publishers.

Most adolescents don't realize this fact. And so, while reading through the magazine, too many are left "wanting" in every sense of the word. They feel less than and endlessly desirous of being someone else.

What a Parent Can Do

- Inform your adolescent about *other* reading material that is more representative of the way real teens look and feel.
- Cut out pictures of normal or slightly heavy girls in magazines and rotate them on the refrigerator door mounted on a piece of paper that has the words, "This Is Beautiful, Too."
- Give your daughter articles on nutrition that speak to clearer skin, healthier hair, stronger bones, and timely sexual development. She may grumble and say, "Oh, not another one!" Give it to her anyway. She'll probably read it.
- Point out great-looking female athletes who have powerful bodies, and discuss the kind of diet she might need to stay "lean and mean."
- Finally, get your daughter some great novels about real girls in which their bodies are simply not the issue! Check with local librarians for suggestions.

TELEVISION, MOVIES, AND THE MUSIC INDUSTRY

The small screen and the silver screen alike are filled with slim and beautiful teens. They have boy problems and girlfriend problems and competition abounds, but always they look great. The drama is distracting, but most adolescents will at least occasionally focus on the clothes, the hair, and the seeming perfection. Unfortunately, the characters are portrayed in normal settings so that the assumption becomes that the characters are normal too. And in some ways they are. Often emotionally, they are right on the money.

But teen actors themselves reflect looks that few girls could achieve. Some girls know this but, it seems, are saddled with another problem: the way in which boys view the female terrain. Girls frequently report that their boyfriend, or just guys, will comment about a model or actress with such shallow phrases as "Wow, is she hot!" So, whether or not they can give themselves a break still leaves them with a very "influential" population that seemingly might not. Of course, some girls feel angry when boys speak this way to each other, but to make statements like "Oh in person she doesn't look like that" sounds too defensive. Pathetic even. Who wants to sound like a bunch of sour grapes?

One 15-year-old put it this way: *"I was sitting with this guy I liked when this beautiful girl came on the screen. He leaned over to his friend and said, 'Man. I'd like her address.' I know he was kidding around—but he also wasn't. I wanted to smack him. Instead I sucked in my stomach."*

What is particularly interesting, however, is that every time a famous star begins to look too thin, the media is all over it. There are very famous names here: Calista Flockhart, Tracey Gold, and Mary-Kate Olsen. Some deny that they have a problem (and maybe they don't), while others are frank in their admission of an eating disorder. But before they do, magazines and magazine shows are awash with questions: Is she or isn't she?

There's a certain excitement that this speculation generates. Suddenly the news is filled with the dangers of anorexia nervosa. Specialists are brought on television, and the question "How could this have happened?" is asked by the very same medium that helped to create the problem. The irony is hard to miss.

As noted in chapter 1, the new makeover shows on television are among the greatest small screen offenders. They shine the spotlight on the imperfect female but do so only in order to point out what needs changing. And then they methodically go about their gruesome tasks. The agenda of "necessary work" might include any combination of dental work, chin implants, face-lifts, and liposuction of the arms, hips, thighs, and chin. Fortunately, they do make it clear that the process isn't fun, but they hardly allow the audience to see any real suffering. And then finally the day comes when she (and we) can look in her mirror.

There are tears—she's joyous, she thanks everyone, she can hardly believe it. Her boyfriend or husband (who claims he'd have loved her the way she was) is suddenly married to a bombshell. He's thrilled. It's his gift, too! Reality comes dangerously close to meeting the Stepford Wives. Now she can step out into the world with confidence and joy. And that's the last we see of her.

We rarely find out that she still has her insecurities, that life isn't changing all that much—many of her inner problems remain—and that probably not everyone in her personal circle is as entranced with what she's done. In fact, they might even be extremely put off.

The message to adolescent girls, who are unfortunately very enthralled with these shows, is that it's perfectly reasonable to go to any length for a head-to-toe makeover. The women are presented as "lucky" for the opportunity. And the subtle message, the one that is never spoken but is there nonetheless, is that it is a woman's natural impulse and perhaps even *responsibility* to *want* to be as perfect as possible no matter what it takes. This is normal. Who cares if it's a veritable torture chamber to get there? It's "natural" to want to meet the standards of conventional beauty.

There is an unforgettable scene in the iconic teen movie *Clueless* in which the beautiful daughter of a prominent litigator is passing by a painting of her mother, who died when her daughter was a little girl. This 15-year-old blithely (and comically?) stops for a moment to gaze at the portrait and then breezily informs her friends that her mother died because of a liposuction surgery that went terribly wrong. Then they turn on the TV.

Apparently, death by beauty is acceptable—even expected, much like the days before penicillin hit the scene and pneumonia was virtually a death sentence. And unfortunately as the news reveals, there have indeed been unexpected deaths resulting from cosmetic surgery. Adolescents rarely hear of these "accidents."

And what about the aforementioned movie *Mean Girls?* What was the ultimate punishment devised for the school's most popular and wicked adolescent? It was convincing her to regularly consume an African "diet" bar that in fact is designed to put *on* weight. The dreaded punishment? *To get her fat.*

And finally, the music scene. The stars look beautiful; they can dance, sing, and sometimes even act. Not all of them are as gifted in the music department as they are in the looks department. But of those young women who are truly gifted with a deep musicality one has to ask, isn't that enough? Can't someone's gift override all other factors? It would seem, in most cases, not. And what sort of message does that send? Certainly one is that "you have to be everything." Of course, there is something titillating about the musical extravaganzas that have singers strutting their stuff in sexy clothes under throbbing lights. But there is no purity to the experience. Our children are watching a show. Not talent. They are not watching what we would wish for them to find within themselves. We want them to honor their strengths—appreciate them and not obsess about more. Who can forget one of the reality performance shows in which a beautiful young woman with an exquisite voice didn't win because she was told she needed to lose weight? Why? Would she sing better? Higher? Clearer?

What You Can Do

- Watch shows and go to movies with your adolescent. Talk to her about your views of certain characters, plots, or subtle messages that you feel underline unreal physical expectations of females.
- If any characters are put down because of their imperfections, explore with your daughter how cruel this is and that there are other ways to view this character that make her more attractive than the beauties in the show.
- Take your daughter to films that show girls with different concerns—sports-oriented characters, for example, that feature images of strong-looking females or girls succeeding in the face of adversity.
- Try to avoid films where ugly ducklings turn into beauties and get the guy.
- Make a list of female stars who are not conventionally beautiful but who have exciting romantic lives or whose success doesn't involve romance at all. During a casual conversation, bring them up saying, "By the way, I know how you love reading about stars. Did you know . . . ?"
- If possible, actively discourage your daughter from watching makeover shows and tell her why. "I hate watching women not like themselves so much that they'd go through all of that to end up looking like everyone else. It's *so* sad." In other words, make it clear that these are *people* deciding to go to drastic measures to change their appearance and that it's worth wondering why they can't just dye their hair, lose a few pounds, or, okay, get a nose job. What's in their heads and hearts that is making them think that a total tortuous makeover is the only way to be happy? Because it isn't. In fact, it's not a way to be happy, period.
- Talk about what boys expect. Much of the reason girls push themselves to be thin is to be attractive to the opposite sex. So a careless comment from a boy such as "Man, I wish I had her" can be very painful. But you might want to suggest to your daughter to either walk away or maintain a sense of

humor that bites back. With a big smile, she might say, "Oh, and you're Justin Timberlake?" Furthermore, if you have sons at home, educate them as to the truth behind all those pictures they are seeing. Their dreams may be dashed, but it might help them focus on a really nice girl whose waist is just a little on the thick side, by "our" standards.

MEDIAGENIC SPORTS

Gymnastics and figure skating are among the most admired and watched sports by adolescent girls. They each, however, confront viewers with a different conundrum. While these two sports display a wide range of strengths and skills, it would seem that each, if admired too much without benefit of insight, could inspire an adolescent girl to place appearance first before athleticism.

Gymnastics is peopled by young women with bodies that are girlish in form. The grueling practice has staved off puberty. This, we are frequently told, is to her advantage. Thin and young wins the day. Admiring the competitors' trim forms can be particularly dangerous for a girl who is facing puberty with untoward anxieties. It can add to the message that staying young is the better way. In fact, as the stars of gymnastics age, the commentary often moves to the increased difficulty older girls have performing up to their peak levels, due to their height and developing bodies. Prepubescent bodies do best. Winning is achieved by women with girlish dimensions. And yet this sport is described as "women's events" at the Olympic level.

This becomes completely absurd when you consider that the average height of a gymnast is around 4'10" with a weight hovering around 92 pounds.

Figure skating presents viewers with another issue. Recent gold medal Olympians in women's figure skating have displayed girlish figures. Take Tara Lipinski, for example, who a few years ago put on a magnificent performance spinning and jumping as if her tiny, tight, and "perfect" little figure belonged in a music box.

The larger issue in figure skating, however, is that for the most part figure skaters present themselves as sensual women on the ice. Competitors are frequently presented in sexualized outfits that strategically cover critical areas, often with feathers and flowers. A material actually called illusion fabric—a filmy material that can appear as if one is wearing nothing—often covers the rest of a figure skater's body. "Skirts" are barely more than tankini briefs, and in pair skating and ice dancing the skaters entwine their bodies together; the barely visible costumes suggest that love, sex, and romance are not only the natural result of such beauty but a necessity to win a competition. The truth is that we forget we are watching *athletes*. What's the talented female figure skater with broad shoulders, shorter legs, and amazing jumping ability to do? And furthermore, the man's job is to "display" this sexualized female. He is there to look good. To look strong. To assure the audience that he won't drop his partner. We check out his muscles. We hardly notice his intricate footwork.

Fortunately, the media *is* beginning to focus more on other females in sports. During the winter there are pieces devoted to females skiers, snowboarders, and more. In warmer weather, we do see marathon runners, swimmers, and tennis players. Sports magazines also now devote more pages to women in sports.

Still, when women compete in basketball, for instance, they receive much less coverage in comparison to the men playing the same sport. And while male athletes are often captured in active poses, women are more likely to be seen staring fetchingly into the camera.

The message? Athleticism is great. But looking beautiful is an important part of being a female athlete.

What Parents Can Do

- Encourage girls to try out every sport, saying, "See which one feels right to you. Where do you feel the strongest?"
- When you see beautiful head shots of pretty athletes, observe the message out loud. "She's not a model! She's a volleyball player for gosh sake?!" Or, if you see a sultry pose from a famous

tennis player wearing a short skirt and tight top, don't be afraid to say, "What? It's not enough that she's a fabulous player? Why does she have to present herself like a sex object? It's insulting to all the effort she's put into her sport. She's an athlete!"

- When your daughter orders her uniform, make sure it's roomy. Tell her, "You want to be comfortable. You want to play the game the best way you can. Tight clothes will hold you back." Make it clear this is about athletic goals, not a beauty contest.

- Stay in touch with your daughter's world. If your daughter wants to wear makeup to a soccer match, let her. Don't send her the message that looking pretty doesn't matter. It does to her. Or she may simply enjoy feeling female. That's different. She's not compromising her performance or self-image with lip gloss. If you argue, you could create a far more problematic situation where, just to spite you, she starts wearing her clothes inappropriately.

- Many pictures of female athletes are posed, often with them not involved in their sport at all. When you come across a picture of a female athlete *playing* her sport your daughter admires, cut it out. Make a collage of several of these photos and give it to your daughter for inspiration. Say something like, "Look how great they look! Athletes can be so beautiful!"

- If there's a copy of the *Sports Illustrated* swimsuit issue hanging around the house, discuss it with your daughter. What does she think of all the male readers staring at these pages? Should women allow themselves to pose so scantily in a men's sports magazine? What harm do they think this does? What message does it send to young girls about sports and beauty?

- If your daughter admires out loud the bodies of the more entertainment-oriented sports such as gymnastics or figure skating, make sure she knows the consequences of maintaining a prepubescent gymnast body or the minimal weight of a figure skater. Also speak to the endless training. These sports have a fluidity that leaves the impression the moves are as natural as rain.

THE POWER OF MEDIA LITERACY

The simple fact is that our children need to be taught to look and listen with a critical eye and ear. If we don't teach this to them, they will become pawns in a game driven by advertising dollars. Depending on your family rhythms, choose the time that works for you. Make the moment humorously formal. You might announce that it's "Media Literacy Time!" Or simply bring a picture or ad to the dinner or breakfast table, pass it around, and say, "So. What's the hidden message? What's wrong with this picture?" Encourage responses that speak to the following:

- Whether the product, if it's an ad, could really deliver on its promise.
- Whether the model in the photo really looks like that in person.
- What kind of photography tricks might have been used.
- Does the girl/woman in this photo look strong or dependent?
- Why is it necessary for the woman to have a man in the picture at all?
- What body types are *not* represented in a group shot?
- How many teenage boys have bodies like that?
- What's a six pack and what kind of workout is necessary to get one?
- The language used in the ad, words like "perfect" or "you've always wanted." What's wrong with these phrases? What do they suggest about us, and how true are they?

Your job is to help your child see these photos as a kind of parallel universe. Sure, these people really do exist but in a world of photo tricks, surgery, stringent dieting, excessive exercise, and more. In other words, it's not *your* world. The real world is full of imperfections. The job of this parallel universe is to convince our adolescents that this doesn't have to be, that they too can be ideal.

But they can't.

They can, however, be the best that they can be, and that ought to be enough.

three
_____

The Role of the Family

> *"I need to lose five pounds."*
> *"I was good today. No desserts."*
> *"I need to go to the gym. I ate too much last night."*
> *"Have I gained weight?"*
> *"That's it. I can't even fit into my clothes anymore."*

All over America, in kitchens, bedrooms, bathrooms, dining rooms, dens, and living rooms, these words are being uttered every day. And not by adolescents who are at risk of eating disorders. They are being articulated by parents and siblings, all of whom have been influenced by cultural messages about the body beautiful. These statements are a reflection of our anxieties. We say them to seek relief from our growing inner tension about our bodies. We say these things to reassure ourselves that we can do something about our weight "problem." And unfortunately we say them, and perhaps this is the most telling, because we are used to saying them. After all, our adolescents are not the first generation to grow up with the idea that fat is out and thin is in. And so we vent. Generally speaking, there's nothing wrong with that.

These aren't bad statements. These aren't misguided statements. These aren't even irresponsible statements.

In fact, given the world we live in, one might think them rather benign, normal, even, horrifically, humorously predictable.

And in many houses they are just that. Worry words, repeated over and over without a serious repercussion to be found. But if you've bought this book, the unfortunate truth is that in your house, these statements could become a problem. While they are nothing out of the ordinary to some ears, to your child they might be something akin to an alarm bell, incessantly warning against the sins of an added pound.

Understand, it is not our purpose to lay *blame* at your feet for any fear of eating your child might now be manifesting. We reviewed in chapter 1 the daunting powers that social and cultural opinions have on each of us. But our purpose here is to call attention to the fact that in your home, to a greater or lesser degree, your attitudes, words, and actions about food will carry "weight"—just as almost certainly your attitudes, words, and actions about anything, be it politics, money, jobs, etc., will also hold some sway over your children. With an adolescent who is already nursing fears about fitting in and looking good, your views about a presidential candidate might be of interest for a minute, but it is your thoughts about your own body image that will linger. Possibly even fester. This is the last thing you want.

Certainly you've heard a lot about the importance of parental role modeling. If you want your children to be polite, be polite yourself. If you want them to reject discrimination, explain why and don't discriminate yourselves. If you want them to feel relaxed about expressing their feelings, then you will have to share some of your own. And perhaps most importantly, if you want them to feel good about themselves, the first step is to put forth your own personal sense of well-being.

How is this done? Simply by talking about the personality traits you value in yourself—the satisfaction you find in your work, the joy of being and having a good friend, and the sense of goodwill you experience when treating others with dignity and respect. And then, of course, turning the tables and speaking of what you value in your children. The emphasis should rest on personal qualities such as kindness, thoughtfulness, a sense of humor, loyalty, and trustworthiness. Well-being, after all, does not come from looking good in a bikini. That's not only fleeting but perilously subject to the opinion of others. It shouldn't even come from a straight-A report card. That too is partially dependent on the outside judgment of others. Well-being, rather, comes from a sense of personal strength, resilience, and pride.

Putting forth this positive sense of self can be particularly difficult for you if your childhood was not a positive one. The more negativity about yourself you carry within, the more readily it can be expressed outwardly. The less satisfied you are with yourself, the more likely you are to fall into a pattern of making self-deprecating remarks. And the more your own sense of self rests on your appearance, the more frequent the temptation to make statements that reveal your concerns about how you look, what you weigh, and the urgency of needing to change some aspect of your body.

In fact, if these insecurities have been with you for a long enough time, you might easily become deaf to the statements you make that reflect your anxieties. If you've been saying "I hate my hips" since you were fourteen, chances are you don't even realize when you say it now. But be assured that your child will. There are some children who for any number of reasons take on a parent's struggle as their own. In other words, your hips become their hips.

So the question becomes, how do you create a home environment that helps your child develop a positive sense of self *and* body image—no matter what your life experience and own internal conflicts? How do you give your child a place to actually learn, know, and feel that what counts most is not losing five pounds in one week.

The answer is threefold:

1. Understand your history and focus on the inherent emotional experiences related to your body image.

2. See the ways in which the past impacts on your present sense of self and the expectations you place on yourself and others.
3. Have a clear and honest perspective on the family dynamics in the home in which your child is now growing up. Strive to see how the dynamics could in some way be impacting your child's genuine sense of self-worth, ability to express herself with honesty, and sense of safety and security.

The first step involves facing your past and the messages that were impressed upon you as you grew up. You will want to do so thoughtfully with an eye toward what you actually felt about these signals. Certainly you can all too quickly say things such as "Oh, my mother always said she was fat," or "As a kid I was chubby and I hated it," or "I always worked really hard to look good because I liked being popular."

But that information is not enough to help you understand yourself and in turn your adolescent. What also matters is your emotional experience, how deeply it impacted on you, in what ways and how to this day you might still be dragging that slightly overweight (if you ever were) child along with you. Because you can be sure that if you are not perfectly clear about the difference between you as a child and the child you are now bringing up, your are likely to impose the past upon the present in ways that cannot possibly be helpful to your child.

> "I could not believe what I did to my 20-year-old daughter the other day. We're standing in the dressing room, and she had on a dress that looked positively stunning on her. Just beautiful. And I said so. But then, unbelievably, I placed my hand on her stomach and pushed in slightly. The saleslady gasped. My daughter gave me a withering look, and I felt like garbage. I couldn't tolerate the sixteenth of an inch her stomach was sticking out? It was, I realized, a habit. I've been doing that to myself my whole life."

MESSAGES FROM THE PAST

Certainly you can remember having a body image. You had mirrors, clothes that fit or didn't fit, a host of people around you making comments here and there, scales, and the pressures of the media. You probably had many thoughts about your body starting from your grade school years.

Were you ever called "pleasantly plump" by a well-meaning relative whom, you disdainfully thought, felt herself clever for avoiding the word "fat"? Did you feel proud as you strutted the beach or lakefront in a bikini, or did you shop for the cutest cover-up you could find, your selection hampered by a sense of unremitting shame? And when you reached into the freezer for a quart of ice cream, did your mother hand you the scoop and say, "Here honey," or did she cluck a bit and warn, "Not too much now," at which point you put the ice cream back?

In other words, what was *your* world like in which your body image evolved?

While there is much you consciously transmit in your home today that reflects your views and values, there is also likely much that is long forgotten or unconscious that plays into the way in which you relate to your family members. Thus, it's important to learn to recognize what drives you. It is the first step in beginning to understand how you became who you are at this moment and to perhaps get in touch with the empathy, understanding, and vision you will need to support your adolescent. Below are some questions to help you begin the necessary self-reflection.

What Do You Remember about How Your Mother Felt about Her Body? How Did You Feel about It?

Did she complain about her clothes not fitting? Did you feel bad for her, or did you think she was being silly because who cares how adults look?

Did she diet incessantly and talk about it constantly? Were you bored or sucked in by the conversation?

Did she seem proud or ashamed of her body?

Did you envy anything about your mother's figure, or were you ashamed?

Did you pray that you wouldn't turn out like your mother?

Did your mother show off her figure, and did that embarrass you?

Daughters can often experience an intense identification with their mothers, and it can be a beautiful thing. It can also be fraught with fears and anxieties. Did you, for the most part, have a benign view of your mother's body? Did you admire it or envy it, or did you in some ways actually dread it?

"My mother had very heavy thighs, though she was quite athletic and the rest of her was slim. She used to try to break up the fat by massaging her thighs. Supposedly in our house a 'fun' activity while watching TV was to massage her thighs for her, 'to break up the fat.' I was somewhere around 8 to 10 years old. At the time it seemed kind of funny, but it also felt a little scary. When I passed through puberty I noticed that my thighs were a little heavy as well, and I spent most of my teens and twenties worrying that they would eventually look like hers. They didn't. But I also worried that if I had a daughter she'd be stuck with those fat, chunky legs my mother tried so hard to massage away."

This mother grew up to have two boys, so she didn't feel that she had to worry about their thighs. When she reached her forties she became obsessed by her own, and while both boys were away at camp she had liposuction for her "saddlebags."

Would she have had the operation if her mother had simply enjoyed her various sports and ignored her "figure flaw"? It's hard to say, but she is quite clear that the anxiety about her own legs began as she concentrated on her mother's. She could recall on many occasions commenting on feeling "fat" to both of her sons. She'd heard this could be a problem with daughters but assumed herself free of risk given that she had sons. That is until she caught her younger son, at age 11, slicing away at a pair of jeans to make very long shorts. When asked why he couldn't just wear his regular shorts, he replied without skipping a beat, "My legs are fat."

HOW DID YOUR MOTHER/FATHER FEEL ABOUT YOUR BODY?

We are perfectly capable of generating our own anxieties about our bodies with the help of the outside world, without a word from our parents. Still, it is at home where we begin to develop our self-worth and sense of what we can be. And, perhaps, what we aren't. Even your well-meaning parents may have had a bit too much to say about your developing body. Perhaps they jumped in too soon as puberty hit to warn you of weight gain and how you might appear in the eyes of others. Maybe your house was tightly controlled emotionally, peopled by disciplined parents and siblings who towed the line, and you were expected to stay as slim and controlled as everyone else. Maybe *you* hovered a bit too closely to an eating disorder. Then again, maybe no one said anything, but you watched your father play tennis twice a week and stay sleek and lean, and sometimes, you thought, he looked at you with disappointment. Consider these questions:

Did either parent say such things as "Are you sure you want to eat that?"

Did your mother reassure you as puberty hit that your body will be changing and not to worry?

Did your father mention that your best friend (who was very thin) was a cute girl?

Did either parent suggest, "Maybe it's time for you to watch your diet"?

Did either parent ever worry out loud that you were not eating enough?

"My mother was a beauty. Slim and tall. My biological father was kind of overweight though handsome, but around the time I turned 9 they

divorced. My mother moved back into the city and soon met a wealthy, rather vain man who took great pride in my mother's looks and his own sleek, aristocratic appearance. I tended to be a little pudgy. At around age 14, feeling unhappy at home and missing my father, who had moved far away, I decided that I really needed a boyfriend. Around this time my mother made a 'loving' remark. It went something like 'Honey, you could have such a lovely figure.' And so I went on a diet. This wasn't too hard, because both my mother and stepfather had gotten very body-conscious. Everything in the house was 'lean,' as they would put it. So I got very lean, which they seemed to think was great. I did too, but I was constipated a lot and very uncomfortable. I felt very lonely—and very hungry. Fortunately, I got a boyfriend who was a bit overweight but so adorable, and he insisted that I needed to put on a few pounds. I was glad, as I was always starving. But I still stayed vigilant for a long time. It wasn't until I was in my early thirties that I allowed myself an average weight."

This mother grew up to have twins, a boy and a girl. Her husband is tall and thin. She is slightly overweight. She'd like to lose a few pounds but talks incessantly about how hard it is to do so. "It's just not my body type," she sighs. "I'm not my mother." Possible translation: "I can't be as beautiful as she was."

Pictures of her mother, however, reveal that while she was tall and lanky, it was her daughter who had the more beautiful face. But somehow to this mother of twins, it was the poundage that counted for true good looks.

HOW DID YOU FEEL ABOUT YOUR BODY?

As we stated earlier, our children are not the first generation to grow up battered into semisubmission by the media. You likely had a great deal of experience as an adolescent dealing with the celebrities and models of the day. But then, of course, if you were not bothered by the media, you still had the mirror, your peers, and your family. How, given all these influences, did you feel about your body?

1. Did you find that you could wear most stylish clothing, or were there many styles that just didn't suit your figure? Did you buy them anyway? How did you feel wearing them?

2. Was shopping for you an exercise in how well you could hide one flaw or another? Did you ever cry in the dressing room and try to convince yourself that the mirrors had to have been hung incorrectly? Did you and your mother argue about what looked good on you?

3. Did you constantly compare your body to that of your friends and find yourself wanting? Were these thoughts with you the moment you entered the front door of school?

4. Did you diet constantly and successfully? Unsuccessfully? Was hunger ever present? What was your experience of hunger? Did you hate it or find it comforting?

5. Were you ever thin enough? Did you ever look in the mirror and think, "That's it. I'm done." Did your mother ever question your "thin" weight?

6. Do you remember how your body changed during puberty? Did anything happen to your body that embarrassed you? Were you proud of what was happening?

7. Were you chubby and insistent that it didn't matter to you, even though it did?

8. Did anyone ever tease you about your body? Did it bring you to tears? Did you go home and study yourself in the mirror for hours?

9. Were you an early or later bloomer? How did you feel about it? Did you want to hide or stand proud? Were you the only one in your group to be late or early with your period? How did that feel? Were you able to talk about it with anyone?

10. Did you often wish that you had someone else's body? Or did you fantasize about a fancy operation in which you could simply reshape your own?

During adolescence, body satisfaction can be frustratingly elusive. It wouldn't matter if you were proportioned as our society would deem "perfect." It's a new body, there are different ones all around you, and it's hard to know what's okay. It's hard to feel that one is good enough or downright attractive.

"My breasts developed early. By the time I was in seventh grade, I was in a size C cup. All the girls stared at me. Almost more than the boys. But the boys, especially the older boys, seemed to think I was ready for something to happen between us. I wasn't. But I couldn't seem to get close to any girls, and so I went along with the boys. I hated my body. My mother was freaked out about my behavior. She was always buying up extra big tops for me to wear so 'things' wouldn't be so obvious. That was another THING. How come she couldn't call them breasts? Was the word bad? I'd sneak out; different boys would call every night. I had no idea what I was doing. It was as if my body had a life of its own. Everyone else seemed to crave it, but I felt as if it were my own personal curse."

By the time other girls caught up with her, this future mother was not in a position to feel relieved. A pattern of disdain and confusion concerning her body had already been set. She still walks with hunched shoulders, embarrassed by her breasts, and she fears that her 10-year-old daughter will go through the same thing. But, of course, her daughter may not if mom can engage her in a positive way and help her feel comfortable with who she is.

HOW ALL OF THESE MESSAGES CAN INFILTRATE YOUR DAUGHTER'S LIFE AND WHAT TO DO ABOUT IT

Most of us can remember our teenage years. Not infrequently we recall them as lonely, disappointing, frustrating, and hurtful. Others might say they were a kick, a blast, a time to feel young and beautiful. Some of us might have felt confident and in control, others insecure and beaten up. The question is, how do we handle our own personal histories when we look at the adolescents in our home? Basically, it plays out in one of three ways:

1. If we had a wonderful teenage life, we want our kids to have that, too.
2. If we had a miserable time of it, we don't want our teenager to get caught in the same trap.
3. And no matter what, if we do not perceive that our beloved children are having or going to have a wonderful time of it, our instinct is to step in and *fix it*. As understandable as this urge is, it is nevertheless fraught with potential problems.

It is your child who has to sort through the slings and arrows of life, with your support, of course, but not at your sole direction. She also needs the emotional tools to handle her disappointments and fears—tools that she will gain through trial and error.

Below is a look of some of the key ways our past impacts on our present selves and our children.

ARE YOU PARROTING YOUR OWN PARENTS?

As with all adolescents, you probably made a private promise to yourself way back that when *you* had kids, you would *not* make some of the mistakes your mother made. You vowed to let your kids have a reasonable curfew. You promised yourself that you'd always knock on their bedroom door. You would make an effort not to stand over them when their friends are over. But you may not have thought in this fashion when your mother constantly suggested that you watch your ice cream intake. You were likely already feeling insecure. You may not have thought, "I'll never do *that* to my daughter," because you were too caught up in your own body image anxieties. Instead you might have thought, "She's right. I hate my body." But it is through the understanding of the emotional impact of your parents' words on you that you will find the empathy to *know* the words you will need to speak to your daughter. If you can recall and feel anew the devastation you might have experienced over remarks you heard (or didn't hear and wish you had) from your parents, you will come that much closer to knowing what to say to your own child. If you can remember how affirming it felt when you were complimented, you might also understand what your daughter needs from you at key moments in her life, and why.

What You Can Do
- Make a list of the statements your mother or father used to make that you felt were critical in any way of your appearance. This includes everything from "Honey, don't you want to put a little blush on?" to "Probably you should stay away from desserts."
- Try to reflect on how each of these comments made you feel. It doesn't matter if then or now you think she had a point. Were you angry? Hurt? Anxious? Ashamed?
- Make a list of all the statements you wish your mother or father had expressed to you as you went through adolescence. These might be as simple as "You look pretty today" or "You have the best sense of humor!"
- If your parents complimented your appearance, try to remember how it made you feel. Do you remember a particular scene as if it happened yesterday, or is it vague? Does it make you smile?
- Given that you don't want to overemphasize looks, but that it is nice for adolescents to feel admired at home, give some thought to how you can compliment her looks without making it sound as if she's achieved the be-all and end-all.
- Consider whether or not you were ever unfavorably compared to a sibling. "Look at how nice your sister looks." Try to remember the many emotions this probably stirred up for you. Jealousy, anger, and resentment are only a few of the possibilities. Certainly you might see more easily now how that can be an easy trap to fall into. You have one child at home who knows how to put herself together and another who seems to

"I'd never felt pretty," Robin reported. "I had a feeling I might be, but neither my mother nor father ever said so. I grew up wondering if maybe all my friends were just fooling me. I don't want to make my daughter feel that being pretty is all that matters, but I do want her to have the confidence of knowing that I think she's a pretty girl. It would have helped me a lot. So now, right before she walks out, I sometimes say, 'You look wonderful.' And then I'm very careful to recognize something else about her later. We may be in the middle of a conversation and I might observe, 'You have such a creative head on your shoulders!'"

be slogging along. It is infinitely more important when you see a disparity like this to avoid trying to *fix it* and instead move toward *understanding* what is happening for each child. We will address how to do this in chapter 4, where we explore the emotional problems with which your child might be struggling.

DO YOU WORRY OUT LOUD ABOUT YOUR OWN BODY AT HOME?

As already noted, most of us do. Again, our children are not the first generation to have been bombarded with media messages or struggle with feelings of insecurity and low self-esteem. You might think that you need to lose a few pounds or have thinner thighs or firmer breasts. Or you may still be that slender girl who once was chubby and can never quite see herself realistically. Whatever it is, you will want to keep your body-conscious feelings to yourself. Share them with a friend. But keep them shielded from your daughter. She will only first look at your body and then begin a close examination of her own.

What You Can Do

- Be careful of "throwaway" statements. Don't say "I feel fat." Say "I need to start eating healthier." Don't proclaim "I was good today. No sweets." Why does abstinence from sugar make a person good? Don't finish up a meal with "Well, tomorrow I better play one hard game of tennis to work that off!" Decide silently to yourself how you will handle tomorrow's food intake.
- When turning down dessert after dinner, simply comment, "I just had a good meal. I don't need any more." You will be underlining what you *have* eaten instead of what you want to stay away from.
- If your daughter sees you holding in your stomach in the mirror, smile and lightly say something like "At some point I'd like to try and lose a pound or two." The point is to project a complete lack of urgency and to help your daughter recognize that needing to lose a few pounds doesn't have to be a matter of the most earnest importance.

DO YOU EXERCISE RELIGIOUSLY, FEELING AN URGENCY TO DO SO?

It's common knowledge that if you want to lose weight, exercise is critical. It's even more important, of course, when you are an adult with a slower metabolism than the one you might have enjoyed when younger. You may also genuinely feel more in control of your appearance if you do exercise strenuously. The problem is that if your daughter watches you run out the door come hell or high water to get to the Stairmaster, saying such things as "I ate too much today," she may figure that she'd better hit the gym too or go for a five-mile run—on a close to empty stomach.

"My mom is very skinny. She's always been really thin. She exercises a lot and skips meals, and when she started yakking at me about my dieting I thought, 'Oh yeah. I should listen to you?' It was hilarious."

In other words, don't expect to be heard if you don't follow your own advice.

What You Can Do
- Pick a time to go to the gym when your daughter is not around.
- If she is around say, "I'm just going to work out for a bit and then do some shopping." Keep the emotions around the exercising at a low ebb. Exercise is simply another thing you are doing in your weekly routine.
- For your own sake and your daughter's, expand the concept of exercise from not just a gym but a nicely paced walk. Invite your daughter to join you, and take that opportunity to speak with her about what's going on in her life. Certainly you can put on sweats and sneakers so it's clear you're out for some exercising, but you can also use such words as "energize" or "pick-me-up." Something like "I feel like I need to get my energy flowing and relax my body. Let's take a walk." The purpose of exercise is to enhance health, not to avoid the dread of extra pounds.
- When eating something healthy, comment that it will give you energy for the gym or a fun game of tennis. This will make it clear that the gym or tennis is not necessarily a way to lose weight but rather something that is simply good for you and that, furthermore, the body needs fuel to make the experience a successful one.

THE FAMILY STYLE

It's impossible to cover all of the messages you might have received at home or the numerous ways in which they might now find their way into your home. And so far, what we've actually dealt with are the words and the emotional atmosphere that were passed down or that could easily be passed down through generations, landing in your home like little grenades just waiting to go off.

But now let's consider something equally powerful. We'll call it the "family style." Every family has one. The style is the emotional tone and pattern of interaction that characterize your family, and while no one thing contributes singly to the birth of an eating problem, there are a few classic family styles that can and often do play into the tendency to become lost in an internal struggle to feel good. We are offering this information not because we think you can or should simply turn around the way in which family members interact in order to create a warm and loving household where no problem can ever erupt. No such guarantee against the development of emotional troubles truly exists. But it is helpful to look at the potential pitfalls of your particular family style so that you might be mindful of when the need may arise to shift behaviors to alleviate the problem. Your family may not clearly fit into any of these categories, but you will likely recognize a tendency toward one characteristic or another. Chapter 4 will explore in fuller detail how these family styles play into the emotional problems your adolescent might be experiencing, but for now you'll want to get a fix on the less constructive aspects of your family life and how they will be experienced by your children. The three family styles are:

Conflict-avoidant family
High-achieving family
Chaotic family

Each of these family styles has particular characteristics that could potentially create a need for an adolescent to find a means to self-comfort—to move inward and express her pain in nonverbal ways, such as dieting. Her body thus becomes the canvas upon which her unhappiness is made known. Certainly, as you will read further on this book, it is likely that if your child is progressing into emotionally anguished territory, it might be wise to see a family therapist. This is *not* because the family is the sole source of blame, but rather because within the context of the family unit there may be some dynamics that are contributing to the problem, and also some untapped strengths that can be harnessed to help aid your child.

At the conclusion of each family style discussion below, we offer three suggestions for how to start moving things in a constructive direction. Still, there is one suggestion that is true in all instances.

If you have trouble with conflict, or only feel good when you're the best, or are struggling with a difficult life circumstance, you as a parent need to take care of yourself. You cannot expect your child to be well if you are harboring unresolved, deep-seated emotional issues of your own. As we have seen, they will all too often seep out into family life in some subtle or even overt way.

You may need to seek out some therapy for yourself (see chapter 9) or some family therapy. The suggestions at the end of each family-style section can work but might be too difficult for you to implement without a bit more understanding of yourself.

THE CONFLICT-AVOIDANT FAMILY

The conflict-avoidant family typically has limited emotional breadth and is tightly controlled. Disagreements, displays of anger or sadness, or even overt bursts of joy are generally suppressed or shunned. On the outside this family may seem peaceful and tranquil, a family in which everyone appears to respect and care for each other. And they very well might, but underneath the calm is often a river of resentment, a sense of isolation, and unhappiness and anger.

Conflict-avoidant parents rarely bicker. If they disagree, discussions end just as quickly as they started or tend to end in no-man's-land. Dialogue trails off. Someone leaves the table. The other might shrug, turn over, and fall asleep. Nothing is resolved. Each member of the couple may on the surface appear contented and satisfied, but beneath this exterior there usually lies a couple awash in unresolved problems. If you spend sufficient time in this household, you can begin to feel the tension.

The children in this family have gotten the message. High emotions, while not exactly frowned upon, are certainly not encouraged or welcomed. Experiencing their parent's inability to enter an argument and see it through to a resolution, the children understand that negative feelings are to be swallowed. These feelings are perhaps even "bad." Maybe these children have tried to bring a problem forward, but with parents who are unused to dealing openly with feelings, the children might have felt put off by well-meaning comments such as "Don't worry. You'll feel better tomorrow." Conflict-avoidant parents will tend to raise conflict-avoidant children. This pattern does not, however, erase conflict. The conflict is simply swallowed and sits inside each member of the family like molten lava.

Patricia, the mother of 15-year-old Becky, had always been mildly depressed. At a young age, she'd lost a brother after a long and grueling illness. Her parents' reaction was to emotionally distance themselves from Patricia and her other sister. Recognizing that Patricia needed help but unable to offer any of their own, they sent her to a psychologist whom she visited all of four times and then stopped, claiming she could handle things herself. Patricia got married in her late twenties to a very kind man, a college professor who preferred to intellectualize any problem. Potential conflicts were not handled emotionally, but rather he would reason things through. This was fine with Patricia, who was in the habit of holding on to herself tightly. Becky had always been a very sweet, calm, intellectually gifted, and apparently flexible child. Any distress she felt she would tentatively express to her mother clearly following the "tone" of the family. And Patricia did listen and respond. She was in fact thrilled that she and her daughter seemed to have such a close relationship, given that hers with her own mother had fallen apart. But in the beginning of eleventh grade, Patricia began to notice that her soft-spoken, obedient, reserved child was losing weight.

Becky is active socially, out in the world, and absolutely being influenced by factors beyond her family. Still, her family's avoidance of conflict and emotional distance are suppressing her desire to just plain express herself. Her family's signal that too much emotional tumult is not a good idea may keep Becky quiet on the outside, but it can't stop her from feeling a great deal of turbulence inside. The question is, where and how is she going to let it out? She may decide to do so by going on a diet. It may feel to her that losing weight is a wonderful way to feel good, even to feel at peace. Now she has something to think about that promises pleasure, a commodity that these days is hard to come by for her. Among the general ramifications of living in this style of family are that children and adolescents

- Do not learn to express their feelings in a genuine way.
- May believe that difficult feelings are better left alone, or that any experience of conflict or anguish is a sign of weakness or inadequacy.
- Can feel misunderstood and alone.
- Might wonder if their feelings are *worth* discussing.
- Might fear making others uncomfortable if they talk.
- May not learn the *language* of emotions because the vocabulary of "feeling" words they have at their disposal is limited.
- May actually be afraid to allow themselves an outburst for fear that the family would somehow fall apart, or worse simply turn away.
- May seek maladaptive ways to self-comfort such as substance abuse or cutting, or eating disorders.

What You Can Do

1. If you recognize your family as being conflict avoidant, try talking about it. Honesty about this dynamic can inspire the honest expression of emotions. "Sometimes I think this family doesn't like to rock the boat. We're all so calm. Doesn't anyone get angry? I know that I do."
2. Model an emotional vocabulary. "Sometimes I get so angry I'm afraid if I start screaming I'll never stop!" "I feel really

upset when you don't call." "I feel hurt when it seems no one is listening to me."

3. Playfully institute a family tradition in which once a week you ask, "Okay. Who got upset this week about something going on in this family and didn't talk about it?" In other words, issue an invitation that says "Let's do something good and talk about the downside of our family dynamic."

THE HIGH-ACHIEVING FAMILY

The high-achieving family might just as easily be called the high-expectations family. Standards are not simply high; they can be impossibly and incessantly high. The parents may themselves be quite successful and expect nothing less from their children. They sometimes have the image of themselves as the "cream of the crop" and simply can't tolerate anything less from their children. It throws their world (and lofty self-concepts) too out of order. These kinds of parents are highly disciplined and driven, accustomed to personal control and expectations of success, and do not allow for failure. Then, too, there are people who appear successful on the outside but who are extremely insecure and self-critical on the inside; they need for their children, as extension of themselves, to prove that they themselves are okay. In both instances the children are seen as reflections of the family. They are genuinely loved but tend not to be seen as people in their own right.

The pattern for many children coming from this dynamic (especially those who later develop eating disorders) is that they strive feverishly to rise to every challenge. They are enormously hard on themselves, naturally falling into line and struggling to meet the expectations of their parents. The difference between what is important to them and important to their parents is often muddied as the children feel an abiding deep need to please. Unfortunately, this can begin to create the somewhat unconscious notion inside the child that it's the achievement that is loved and not the child herself. She has to present as the others in her family do or she won't be valued. In these families, the child who falls into extreme dieting is often striving to assert self-will and breakaway independence. The eating disordered behaviors are a masked expression of defiance or a discipline and restraint that she secretly feels is otherwise lacking or deficient in her life.

No matter how one refers to this sort of family, at some point, typically during the adolescent years when the pressures from the outside world—socially, sexually, and academically—must be confronted, the child might begin to feel overwhelmed. Frightened by what is expected from her and feeling unable to share with parents who seem to only want to see *results*, the child may turn her growing need to control something, anything, inward. And so the dieting assumes many functions, unbeknownst to all.

Dana's parents were both graduates of prestigious schools and highly successful in their work. Her father, a music industry executive, had come from a very well-to-do, loving, and supportive family. Her mother, the CEO of a publishing company, was the product of a lower-middle-class home in which she received little overt affection from either parent and had worked hard to get where she was in life. Dana, an extremely bright child, was the oldest of three daughters. As a young child she was a devoted figure skater—something her parents supported and encouraged. Dana had talent and seemed to enjoy the discipline of skating very much. She was also an excellent academic student, and her parents took extraordinary pride in the parent-teacher conferences where they would receive nothing but glowing reports. Dana was, to them, a "golden child." Both parents regularly told their daughter how proud they were of her accomplishments. Occasionally, when a less than stellar grade would come in, they'd sit her down and discuss it, but then they'd put it behind them.

Nan, her younger sister by not quite two years and a very bright girl, also took up figure skating. As it turned out she had exceptional talent, and while her parents encouraged each girl equally, it was apparent to

Dana that her sister would soon outshine her in the ice arena. When puberty hit and Dana's body began to change, it was clear that she was having trouble adjusting her skills. Also, her body type was no longer the classic delicate frame of a skater. Meanwhile, her sister began winning competition after competition. Dana's mother, who had left her high-powered position when her third daughter was born and was now establishing a consulting business, began shepherding Nan from competition to competition, thrilled at the level of her middle daughter's success.

Dana seemed to take this in stride, and, in fact, both parents noticed that she turned even more intently to her studies. Straight A's had become a matter of course. Her room, which had all her life been something of a mess, suddenly became a focus of Dana's attention. It was suddenly extraordinarily orderly. The bed, in fact, was made so tightly and the pillows arranged so artfully that Dana's mother would chuckle over her eldest daughter's admirable ability to keep everything "so together." When Dana entered high school her grades for the first semester slipped just a little, and she seemed to panic. Both parents patiently explained that such a dip is very commonplace, but Dana did not seem soothed. And so she began eating. Nan, a solid B student, which was fine with her parents, meanwhile was giddily moving up in the figure skating ranks.

In the middle of ninth grade Dana, who had during and after puberty gained a few pounds, announced that she was going to go on a diet. Both parents, admitting that she'd gotten a bit "plump," were pleased to hear this. Her mother offered to keep low-cal foods in the house. Again Dana's parents were pleased over their daughter's desire to be the best that she could be. And so Dana began dieting. But having reached a nice, trim size, she didn't want to stop. Dana's mother began to fear for Dana's health and started arguing with Dana at every meal. Dinnertime became a marathon struggle that ruined everyone's appetite and usually found Dana running from the table—after having eaten practically nothing.

Dana's parents had unwittingly fallen into the trap of applauding their daughter's many accomplishments instead of their daughter herself. Aware of the expectations they had of her, Dana had worked hard to fulfill them. Her mother, who was not a spontaneously warm person, always seemed to come alive when Dana performed well. When Nan's own talents made themselves evident, Dana's already compromised sense of self-worth began to plummet. Highly competitive, Dana fought to stay on top of her skating, but her genetics superseded her efforts. She began to feel out of control. Whereas before everything she touched turned to gold, now, as puberty hit, it felt as if her stature in the family, and in the world, had begun to fall away. And so, unable to put these feelings into words, Dana tried to gain back some control.

In the high-achieving family, children and adolescents

- Begin to believe that it's what they *do*, not who they are, that counts.
- Often don't know who they are beyond their accomplishments.
- May be completely intolerant of their imperfections.
- May unconsciously be extremely angry at their parents for expecting so much.
- May begin to despise themselves for not being able to deliver.
- May not discuss these feelings because when they do, they are often "encouraged" with comments like "We know you can do it" that lead her to think "What if I can't? Will you still love me?"

What You Can Do

1. Begin to redefine for yourself the definition of a successful child. It isn't in the A report card or the blue ribbon. It's the child who is proud of herself for both who she is and what she can do. Success isn't necessarily being at the top of her class; it is enjoying the excitement of learning.

2. If you see your child working hard to "be the best," tell her in no uncertain terms that it isn't necessary. In fact, being the best is a very stressful and lonely place to be, as there is no

place to go but down! This will not, as you might fear, lead to a child who heaves a sigh of relief and then consistently wants to party. But it will give her a chance to see that she is honored for who she is and not what she can do.

3. Be honest about the pressure she might have experienced coming from you. "We think we've been pushing too hard. That's wrong. We know you're a smart kid, but you're not a grade machine." These kinds of words not only let her see that making a mistake is human (EVERYONE makes them!) but also expresses your respect for her.

4. Encourage loose, unstructured fun times. If she's been studying a good part of the afternoon walk in and say, "Enough! Let's go to the movies. You must be exhausted!" The point is to project the notion that feeling well is as important as doing well.

THE CHAOTIC FAMILY

The chaotic family has many faces. Thematically, however, these families share a number of qualities. Generally, the communication between family members is highly inconsistent. The parents may not get along, or a family tragedy such as a parental illness may have disturbed the balance of the family. An ugly divorce, a complicated meshing of families from a remarriage, substance abuse, or a disturbed family member are some of the reasons this chaotic state can take hold. What results are feelings of anger, sadness, confusion, and resentment that are finding expression in either family arguments that have nothing to do with the real problem or in a general state of debilitating tension. In *all* cases the child who exhibits problems with eating is trying to find a calm or distracting place in the maelstrom raging around her.

A child coping with this sort of family dynamic is likely to feel that there is no real safe haven in the family. After all, no one is taking hold of things and putting things right. To the contrary. Everyone seems to be contributing in their own way to the daily confusion in the family. Some children may do their best to simply escape the house as much as possible. Others might feel a sense of responsibility to stay and try to bring order. A child may perceive a parent as needing her support (and with good reason, as this parent may treat her like a friend upon whom she can lean) and begin to view herself as powerful, in control, and the one above it all. Unfortunately, deep inside this girl's childhood and adolescence are being trampled upon. She may have a sense of what she is feeling but is afraid to express herself. She may have little sense of what is going on either around her or inside her but has created a story that works to keep her afloat. She may decide that in this world where everything has gone awry, *she alone* can and will take care of herself. And depending on all the other factors in and outside her home, she may turn to her body as the canvas for both painting a picture of order and hiding a quickly growing chaotic internal life.

Cassie, age 16, is a beautiful girl. Jane, her mother, walked into this first therapy session perfectly coiffed, her blond hair bouncing, and smiling. Cassie was equally well-groomed. Her mother had brought her because, as she stated, "Divorce is difficult on children. Especially only children." Jane spoke quickly and with a singsong voice. She offered the information that she had been anorexic as a teenager, and while she is still quite thin, she described herself as "still a little neurotic about it, but really just fine." Jane and her husband, Cassie's father, had divorced two years earlier. During this trying time, Jane had leaned on Cassie constantly for support, something that Jane repeatedly stated "wasn't a good idea, but my daughter was such a good friend." In response to this, Cassie smiled proudly. A few months ago, however, Jane had announced that she was remarrying. He was an architect with two children of his own. The wedding took place almost immediately, and Cassie and her mother promptly moved into his house.

But things did not go smoothly. Jane discovered that her new husband was something of a workaholic and given to staying out late at night with his friends "to have a drink and unwind." "He likes to act like he's still single," she reported ruefully. His own divorce was years ago, but his children were upset and resentful over the speed with which Cassie and her mother had moved in. Again, Jane had begun leaning on Cassie, at one point crying on her shoulder with the words, "What have I done? Do you think this is a mistake?" Cassie reported replying, "Don't worry. You'll work it out. Things take time." Her mother told this story with a mixture of great pride and embarrassment as she recognized the parent-child role reversal. Cassie again sat beside her beaming mother. Jane continually tucked Cassie's wavy hair behind her ear, straightened out her daughter's skirt, or whispered incessantly such things as "Stop picking at your nails," or "Sit straight," or "Blow your nose."

Cassie herself reported feeling faint now and then. She explained that she exercised two hours a day and was a straight-A student. She forthrightly proclaimed that she was heading for Princeton and that she intended to be a U.S. Senator so that she could make some laws that "made sense." When asked how things were going at home, she would regularly reply, "Oh fine. I don't let anything bother me." And then as if to almost tease her therapist, Cassie would recount all manner of incidents that must have threatened her sense of self-worth, but she did so in a tone similar to what one might use to recite a recipe: Her mother never allowed her to leave her room in the morning unless her bed was perfectly made, including fluffed pillows and hospital corners. Cassie frequently made plans with her friends with her mother's permission only to be told at the last minute that it wasn't going to fly for any number of reasons, ranging from "It isn't safe" to "I need you to watch your new little sister." None of this, according to Cassie, was all that problematic. Even coming home from a week in Florida for a visit with her grandparents to find her belongings in a shambles as she was being moved into her stepsister's room to allow for a home office wasn't so bad. "I told them it wasn't fair," Cassie reported smoothly. "But then the whole thing blew over. I got a new bed, sheets, and comforter."

Cassie was adamant that she did not need therapy and that in fact it was her mother who needed some attention (the latter part of her state-

ment being entirely true). Previous to these joint sessions, her mother tried several times to get Cassie to therapy but at last gave up, saying with a sad smile, "My daughter. She's always been strong-willed."

At this point her strong-willed daughter was 5'1" and weighed 92 pounds, and when it was brought to Cassie's attention that she looked rather thin, she shrugged and casually said, "You should see what I eat for dinner." When asked if she ever throws up after a meal she replied, "Well, doesn't everyone once in a while? You know. When you eat something that wasn't good and kind of makes you sick?"

Cassie was clearly struggling to cope with a chaotic situation. Her mother was battling her own inability to face conflicts, not to mention a problem with body image and food. She was feeling as if she'd lost control of her own life and was depending on her daughter to be a kind of anchor. Cassie's father lived a plane ride away. He noticed his daughter's weight loss and was concerned but didn't want to argue with Jane, whom he found to be too "in your face." Cassie was living with a difficult stepfather, and with stepsiblings who resented her presence. Cassie was suspiciously sanguine about her father's limited role in her life. "Some men aren't meant to be fathers," she philosophized. Cassie had clearly decided that the best route within this chaos was to take on the role of the one who could rise above it all. She was strong. She was in control. She had plans. Nothing bothered her because she was great at everything she tried. To boot, Cassie was living in an affluent community where the other girls her age were in massage parlors, beauty salons, and gyms almost as often as they brushed their teeth. All of her friends worried incessantly about their weight. Cassie felt herself to be in good and normal company. And so she dieted, purged now and then (doesn't everyone?), and felt almost nothing about anything. Ever.

As with the girls in the other families, Cassie is on the brink; an eating disorder is precariously close to blossoming.

In chaotic families, children and adolescents

- May react to the confusion at home by pulling inward and becoming almost invisible.
- May find themselves in an inappropriate parental role, since the adults do not seem able to manage their problems.
- May push aside their own anger or depression, as there appears to be no room for it or any hope of it being addressed constructively.
- May insist that they hardly notice the mayhem because it doesn't effect them (in psychological terms, they disassociate).
- Have no idea how to productively communicate real feelings because everyone around them can't handle or speak about their own feelings except in destructive ways.
- Imagine themselves impervious to pain and thus begin to see their own problems as normal. After all, everyone diets—a lot.

What You Can Do

1. Be clear about boundaries in the family. When times are tough, parents can act like children and children can feel that they need to act like adults. Your child needs to know that she can still depend on you and that it is not her responsibility to keep you together.
2. Talk about the chaos. Don't pretend that it isn't there. Wait for a moment when you are not feeling highly emotional, and then put it out there. "Let's talk about what's going on in the family." Tell her how you are feeling (briefly), and ask her to do the same. Make it clear that the unrest isn't a secret and ought to be dealt with openly. It's the only way for everyone to get through the tough times.
3. If your child insists that she's fine, you can't say she isn't fine; however, you can find other ways to let her know that you realize she's struggling. She may not respond immediately, but it's a way to crack the door open so that when she's ready to talk it won't be so difficult to begin. "It's hard to believe you're

fine! Things are so confused around here." Or "Well, maybe you're fine, maybe you're not, but if you want to talk just let me know." Your child will not mind that you don't believe her. She might only say that she does.

This chapter has clearly been about how our histories affect who we are and how the ways in which we live our lives influence the lives of those we love. The reflection of our histories can be found in things we say (and don't say) and feel (and don't feel). It is also present in how we behave, experience ourselves, see others, and handle the ups and down that life inevitably brings. Remnants of the patterns of our own families of origins can also often be found in our present family life. As the last part of this chapter illustrated, there is much to understand about the way a family style impacts on how our children might develop and address their own problems.

The next chapter takes these issues a step further, honing in more closely on the emotional problems many children experience as they suffer with an eating disturbance or when teetering on the brink of an eating disorder. Keeping everything you've learned so far about genetics, the effects of the media, the social environment, and the histories we as parents always bring to the proverbial table, now we are going to examine not so much the problem with eating, but the different emotional issues and problems that work behind the exhilaration of weight loss. These issues are, in a sense, the highly personal engines behind the need to diet. Remember, an eating disorder is not really about food at all, but rather the feelings that food issues are masking. By understanding the emotional underpinnings of your child's flirtation with an eating disorder, you will be better able to identify the true problems you must face up to with your daughter.

four

The Emotional Undercurrent

Clearly, a problem with eating is likely to exist within the context of broader problems related to emotional well-being. The psychological settings, however, will differ widely. Thus one girl who is prone to extreme anxiety may be particularly vulnerable to fears of weight gain as puberty sets in. She may worry that she simply isn't quite thin enough. In this case the trait at the root of the apparent problem with eating is one of anxiety. But another girl might have a chunky body type and self-esteem issues that develop from being teased. As the years go by, her self-perception worsens until she feels weighed down by depression. Her logic is that she has to fix the way she looks or she'll have to seek protection by hiding. In this case one might conclude that her naturally heavy body type, unstable self-worth, and social surroundings gave birth to a depression that in turn inspired her intense body image issues.

The point to be stressed is that eating disordered behaviors should never be seen as an isolated matter. Rather, it is very important that we consider the possibility that the excessive dieting is part of other complex issues with which our children might be struggling. We need to understand the various psychological problems and character traits that exist within our children along with this problem of being just a little too thin. We need to appreciate the emotional pressures faced by adolescents as they move through puberty. You can't expect your daughter to gain back weight or to reduce her extreme dieting if no attention is paid to her low self-esteem, or high anxieties about life, or depression, or intense need to achieve perfection. Dieting problems and the psychological life of your child are entwined.

If your daughter is to find the strength to confront and fight her fears about herself, you and she both have to have a basic understanding of what is going on for her emotionally, genetically, and developmentally. This knowledge will not only help you reach your daughter in powerful new ways but will also give your daughter an opportunity to see her problem with weight worries as something bigger than a simple desire to be thinner.

The plain truth is that without this intellectualized understanding of the deeper and broader problems that potentially form a kind of nest for the development of eating disorders, you cannot begin to address your daughter's dieting problem in an effective manner.

In past chapters we've looked at the influence of media both psychologically and socially as well as the role played by the generational family dynamics. These many influences shape your daughter's emotional life. But now the problems need to be identified and understood in terms of their *impact* on your child.

This chapter will help you understand the critical passages your child will travel that can impact on her sense of self, emotions, body image, and optimism about life. It will help you see the potential psychological problems that disrupt this passage as well as the danger signals that significant problems are developing. How do you sort through the emotional issues and, when you can identify them, what can you do about them?

Certainly outside help may become necessary, and we will take this up in chapter 8. But for now, what can your contribution be?

A very good starting point is to consider the impact of puberty. Most potential eating disorders surface around this time, and so it is important to take a detailed look at the challenges this critical time can pose for your adolescent. It is easy for us to think of the dawning of womanhood as "exciting" for our daughters. But in truth, for most girls, it is a far more complicated passage than that.

PUBERTY

Puberty marks a sequence of profound biological, psychological, and physical changes that are reflected in dramatic shifts in a child's appearance.

In girls, the ovaries quickly increase their production of the female hormone estrogen. In boys, the testes increase production of androgens, especially testosterone. These hormones are responsible for the sexual maturation that takes place over approximately two to three years.

These hormones also stimulate the appearance of secondary sex characteristics, physiological signs of sexual maturity that don't directly involve the reproductive organs. For girls these include breasts and hips, and for boys broad shoulders and facial hair. In both sexes, changes occur in the voice, the texture of the skin, and the development of pubic hair. During puberty girls and boys gain roughly 20 percent of their adult height and 50 percent of their weight. Their skeletal mass, heart, lungs, liver, spleen, pancreas, various glands, and sexual organs (including the uterus in girls) double in size.

When girls are about 10 years old they develop breast buds, and some even begin to grow pubic hair. A first menstrual period can appear anywhere from a year to two or three years later, accompanied by the development of hair under the arms and sometimes on the upper lip. Girls also develop a distinctly female smell during puberty. Their sweat glands become more active, and their perspiration begins to smell like adult sweat. As their vaginal lining thickens, it begins to produce secretions that also have a distinct odor. At this stage of puberty the texture of the skin begins to change, and the oil glands become more active, leading to pimples and blackheads.

By the time girls have finished puberty they will have significantly increased their weight. Changes in weight of up to forty and fifty pounds over a period of several years is not at all unusual. This weight is added to all areas of their bodies in the form of fat, especially their breasts and hips. Fat gain at this time plays a very important role in regulating the hormones estrogen and progesterone, which are necessary for menstruation and pregnancy. For women, the percentage of body fat is one and a half to two times greater than it is for men.

I HAVE A FEELING WE'RE NOT IN KANSAS ANYMORE

For many girls, the experience of puberty can be sudden and a bit frightening, like getting caught up in a tornado and then landing in Oz. In fact, much like the yellow brick road, the journey is fraught with dangers. Or so it seems to them. And the truth is, much like Dorothy, some girls can feel that they'd be just as happy to go home again.

But of course they can't. Instead, they are now being called upon to use their hearts, brains, and courage to navigate a whole new world. They look different, they feel different, and there are, it seems, a bewildering and confusing mass of new rules and expectations that they have to juggle. "You're becoming a woman!" is the unwelcome line they often hear. But what, they must think, does that actually mean? And why do I still feel like and sort of want to be a kid? The simple answer is that emotionally they *are* still children, but the changes in their bodies and the assumptions that go with those changes seem to overlook their emotional state.

Suddenly girls are supposed to have a new, more mature attitude toward school. Friendships with boys are now becoming very complex, and new rules and warnings are coming at them from every front. Teachers expect different study habits; parents expect increased independence but often behave so overprotectively that it's hard to know what they want; relationships with girlfriends can take on a rudely competitive aspect; and boys are suddenly a preoccupation that knows no bounds. This is a time when girls and boys too are supposed to begin to "individuate"—a term used by psychologists that refers to the process of pulling away from parents for the purpose of exploring who they are and what is unique about their ideals and values. This process is what gives fuel to the experimentation that can often drive parents crazy, inspiring their efforts to try to hold their children back. It is also the time in which teens learn to form the kinds of friendships and intimate bonds they will need throughout their lives. Confidences now are being shared more with peers rather than parents. But not all young teens are truly prepared for all of this, even if their bodies say they are.

Becky had been extremely close to her mother. She'd always wanted her approval, but more than that she only felt okay when she'd recited to her mother "everything that happened that day." It was as if she needed to double check that her world was indeed safe. Becky seemed to get her sense of being okay from her mother, and her mother, an anxious woman, enjoyed the role. She liked the closeness.

At age 15 Becky got her first boyfriend. Over the course of a few months she became extremely attached to him, switching her allegiance and dependence onto him. Becky's mother was able to tolerate this but would on occasion and by her own admission try to pull Becky back to the confessional relationship that had been theirs. That summer, eight months into the relationship, Becky's boyfriend and his family moved away. Becky was left completely out of balance. She could not quite return to her mother, but the alternatives were not clear.

A girl with a strong dependent aspect to her personality, Becky felt lost, confused, and frightened. She began to obsess about her body, complaining for the first time that her legs were too "thick." Her mother was perplexed, but Becky was determined. She began to diet and after a ten-pound loss simply didn't want to stop. It was as if she had found a new "entity" to which she could attach herself. Only this time it wasn't a person. It was her relationship with her body. Individuation had definitely gone awry.

It is in the midst of this swirl of psychological upheaval that a new and harsh pressure to look good and fit into the popular ideal of female beauty sets in. Unfortunately for the girl emotionally unprepared for puberty, the same fat that biology dictates is a necessary aspect of healthy female development is now seen as an enemy she must engage in battle. Instead of feeling proud of their rounded shape, many girls feel conflicted. The changes are exciting, but how do the results measure up to the high bar society seems to have set? They can begin to feel as if their bodies either fail to measure up or are simply out of control. They may ruminate over what is happening to them and feel lost as to how to cope with it. Since their bodies are the most *obvious* sign of change (many social expectations being more subtle, though no less frightening), many girls focus their anxiety on their changing shape. Again, their bodies thus become the canvas for all manner of struggles they are experiencing.

It is also around this time that girls can begin to see their bodies as pieces of a puzzle instead of a whole. They may think that their breasts are fine but that their behinds are too large. Their thighs may be thin, but their breasts are too flat. Individual pieces of themselves become "areas to work on." Caught in this often ongoing systematic body assessment, it is hard for them to step back and take in the whole picture.

Faced with a need to do something to manage this angst, girls begin to carve their bodies up into its parts, giving each area—hips, thighs, breasts, waist, stomach, etc.—different grades. A little too often there is a failing grade or two.

"I worried a little about being a little chubby during puberty. I started to notice that the tops of my thighs were getting fat, but my mother told me

Jenny walked into her therapist's office wearing a skimpy top that showed off her well-developed breasts and a pair of tight blue jeans that clearly outlined slim legs and a gentle curve to her hips. Jenny was only partly happy. "What's with my behind?" she asked. "I hate it. And my legs. They're still too fat." She looked at the therapist with frustration. "What am I gonna do about my bottom half?" Clearly, societal values were kicking in here, as even this girl, distressed about her changing body, had nothing negative to say about her chest.

that would change when I was 'finished developing.' But she was wrong. I waited and waited, but the fat stayed there. The rest of my legs are nice. My breasts are kinda flat. My waist is thin. But those lumps of fat are driving me crazy. Every morning I get up and pray before I look in the mirror that they'll be gone. They never are."

Each body change that occurs is often focused upon intently. But whatever is imperfect seems to count most.

ARRIVING IN KANSAS EARLY

For some girls puberty arrives early. For others the arrival is delayed. Whether they are at one end of the developmental spectrum or the other, these girls will often feel that they stand out. This is particularly true for those who mature early. They appear more sophisticated and thus are often treated as if they are older. This is very difficult when it comes to boys who see them in more sexualized ways. Anxious parents will often mishandle this situation, seeking to help their daughter draw less attention to her sexually maturing body. They want to protect her, forgetting to help her feel proud and confident in her new shape. Often, a parent's first instinct is to help her daughter "hide" the facts. As a result, instead of feeling excitement and ease about their changing form, girls can instead feel embarrassment and shame, and they may deal with this discomfort by encoding their feelings in the language of fat. "I need to lose weight" often means "I don't like myself." They may also begin to date prematurely and sadly, in order to receive some affirmation that they are okay, run the risk of being sexually active when they are not ready.

The most important thing any parent can do is communicate the idea that physical and sexual maturation is a normal, healthy, and natural part of growing up. Too many of us, perhaps due to the way our parents ignored our developing sexuality, have relegated it to the drawer marked "Say the Bare Minimum" or "Move On." But that is not what adolescent girls need.

What You Can Do

- Open up the subject of menstruation before your daughter begins it. As soon as you can arrange some time to be alone, in a relaxed tone, let her know what will be coming. You needn't tell her how to *feel* about or *interpret* it. "It's so exciting" may not be her experience. It probably doesn't adequately describe your experience either. "You're becoming a woman" might frighten her. Keep your comments to the facts—what she will notice—as changes that are a part of development unfold.
- Don't simply say, "I'm happy to answer any questions." She won't know where to start. Instead, and this may mean that you need to do a little reading up on the subject, offer information. This will make it clear that you really are ready to share; that this phase of life, although difficult in some ways, is predictable and manageable; and that discomfort is also quite expected. You will, of course, also want to make the connection between menstruation and pregnancy, both as a

gentle warning and a reassuring and wonderful indication of
the female body's potential.

- If you feel a little uncomfortable talking about it, say so. Otherwise, she may think the subject really ought to be a secret. "It's a personal thing that people sometimes feel awkward with," you might say, "but it's a wonderful and important part of growing up, and I want to make sure I'm helpful."

- Check the library or bookstore and see what books are available. Bring one or two home that seem the most friendly and informative. Offer to look them over with your daughter, or if she prefers let her take them into her room alone. See the "Further Reading" list for an idea of what books to start with.

- Mark her first period by taking her out to lunch or with a kind of special private talk. Underlining the significance of the changes taking place in a personal and pleasurable way is a very positive strategy.

- If her experience with menstruation leaves her crampy and moody, explain what's going on and be sympathetic. But don't do so with an attitude that communicates the age-old concept of menstruation as "the curse," whether you are joking or not. "Isn't it horrible?" should be replaced with "I was just like this when I was your age. I know it hurts. Most girls and women feel this way. It will pass. It's the hormones. How nice to know that your body is doing exactly what it's supposed to do."

- As the added weight begins to appear, be open to your daughter's concerns. Statements such as "Oh, don't worry about that! It's normal. It's great!" won't help. It's not normal for her, and she may not think it's great. Saying so will only shut your daughter down. Instead, if you notice that she seems distressed, try to draw her out. "Your body is taking on a new shape. How are you feeling about this?" If she reveals that she doesn't like it and that she feels she's getting fat, acknowledge her feelings. "I know you've lived with one kind of body for a long time. Now you're growing into another unfamiliar one. But you know, while I realize it's 'fat' to you right now, I hope you begin to see that what you're looking at is the development of a woman's body. Give yourself time to get used to it— you're looking beautiful to me."

- Share your own experiences as an adolescent. How did you feel? Were you embarrassed about anything? "I used to worry that people would know I had my period because of a pimple on my forehead." Were you proud of the changes in your body, or did you initially experience confusion? Most importantly, describe the emotional experiences you had as they evolved. At first perhaps you hated the changes, then you became kind of interested in what was happening, then excited, and then thrilled at the new kinds of clothes you could wear. In other words, underline the *process* taking place.

- If she immediately tries to start dieting, let her know that it's not a healthy time to do so, but in a way that respects her need to control some aspects of her bodily changes. "Honey, you don't want to deprive your body of nutrients now because your body is healthy and telling you it's time for hormonal and sexual changes to begin. If you're anxious about it changing too quickly or drastically, let's at least talk about what you should eat to keep the process going. If you aren't careful, you could stop your natural development and things in your body—like your bones and muscles—could grow weak."

THE DIET AS SELF-MEDICATION

When people are depressed, anxious, afraid, or angry, they often attempt to self-medicate. They might turn to alcohol to soothe their frayed nerves, calm their fears, and reduce the feelings of hopelessness or loneliness that haunt them on a daily basis. It's a sort of anesthetic.

Recreational drugs are also often used to hide from painful feelings. The "high" brings quick relief. Feelings of being powerful and in control also often permeate a drug experience, but of course it's an illusion. Still, the initial pleasure it brings and the relief it can offer, as with alcohol, can lead to an addiction. Why, after all, should we have to continue to feel so bad if we can feel so good?

Obsessive dieting can serve very much the same function as alcohol and drugs. It is a way of soothing fears, anxieties, depression, and other feelings that are difficult to cope with such as despair, loneliness, and confusion. An adolescent may be using dieting to feel as if she is gaining control of her life, which otherwise she experiences as unmanageable. She may diet to ease the conflicts she has between remaining a child and growing into a young adult. She may use dieting to reduce depression by telling herself, "Look how successful I am at this!" Obsessive dieting can pull her away from the painful thoughts that would otherwise wear her down. "Everyone hates me" is replaced by "Today I will only eat a small salad, with lettuce, cucumber, and celery, and one apple. No, maybe half an apple. I'll drink eight glasses of water, and not soda," and on and on it goes.

In all probability your daughter is wrestling with some aspects of depression or anxiety. Since there are different ways to experience these emotional problems, it is important to understand in what ways your daughter is struggling. You will best be able to help her if you can recognize the particular face of her depression and anxiety. And stepping in early rather than waiting to act is crucial, because the cycle is a vicious one: The more she diets, the more alienated she becomes and the greater the pull into more frantic weight control. It stands to reason that the sooner you reach a sense of what the source of her trouble is, the easier it will be to talk to your daughter and find her the appropriate help.

DEPRESSION AND ITS RELATED FEATURES

Depression actually has many different connotations. Most generally, it refers to feelings of sadness, hopelessness, and an inability to experience real pleasure. Sleeping may be disrupted, and fatigue is constant. There is often either a marked decrease or increase in eating and often a significant social withdrawal. Problems with concentration may occur, and a depressed person can frequently be tearful and not easily able to identify the specific reasons for her unhappiness. Depression can be triggered by a single, sometimes stressful event or can seemingly build on its own.

Depression can arise from genetic vulnerability to low moods or can result from specific difficult life experiences and self-perceptions. Some young people identify at least part of the source of their pain, but others cannot, at least not while they are in the midst of eating disordered behavior. When asked if something is bothering them, the replies are often something like this:

> "I just feel like everyone is driving me crazy, and I wish they'd leave me alone. It makes me furious."
>
> "Well, all the kids hate me. I don't know why. But that has nothing to do with me wanting to be thin."
>
> "No one understands anything in this family. I'm fine. It's everyone else who is blind."

In general, teens have a hard time connecting problem eating with anything other than the idea that being really thin makes them feel better. But of course, if you were to take a close look at the above statements, you might hear indications of what's playing out beneath the surface. The first speaker is clearly feeling a great deal of stress and is experiencing intense anger. The second is likely feeling painfully lonely and rejected, and the third may be experiencing isolation within the family.

In addition, teenagers commonly and defensively look at their peers as the ultimate litmus test that they are fine rather than explore what's truly happening to them emotionally. They will say things like this:

> "There is nothing wrong with me. I'm fine. I look like everyone else."

"You think I don't eat? You should spend a day with Jenna."
"This is the only way to attract boys."

All of these statements are often delivered in a flat tone, as if it's an open-and-shut case. The reality is that this is likely a child who is feeling a deep need to fit in, and one who is extremely vulnerable to the messages of the times.

In all cases each of these girls is quite probably dealing to varying degrees with insecurities, low self-esteem, and a deep need to be loved and admired.

Recognizing the Symptoms of Depression

- Tearfulness. She seems to start crying in response to the slightest provocation.
- Difficulty sleeping. She doesn't fall asleep easily and seems unrested upon awakening.
- Less socializing or a tendency to isolate. She reaches out less and is clearly being sought after less. The phone isn't ringing, and weekends include few if any peers.
- Angry outbursts. Confused and scared by her own unhappiness, she may suddenly have a tantrum for no apparent reason.
- Substance abuse. She may reach for alcohol or drugs to both stave off bad feelings and keep her away from food.
- Unemotional. She may seem completely unemotional. Nothing riles her at all.
- Lack of pleasure. There is less smiling, laughing, and general animation. Hobbies and routines that used to provide some fun are dropped.

Feeling Inadequate

Feelings of inadequacy are not that uncommon in adolescents. As we have noted, they've undergone (or are undergoing) dramatic changes physically and emotionally, new expectations outlined by others have been presented in abundance, and there is a nagging sense that they cannot keep up with what is happening to them. It's too sudden. Too overwhelming. One minute her friends are comparing jewelry and the next breast size. Only a year ago she might have thought of boys as largely obnoxious and stupid, and now she may be noticing some furtive glances and not be able to understand her own excited but confused feelings. The desire to enjoy independence both in thoughts and actions may be confusing and challenging at the same time, especially for those children who have excelled at being "good girls" and following the rules.

Low Self-Esteem

"Low self-esteem" is a phrase that is frequently used though not often fully understood. The phrase seems to imply that it comes in the same size and shape for everyone so that it hardly requires definition. But this is not so. In general, low self-esteem points to a person's poor sense of self-worth or value. However, this may not be true in every area of a person's life. She may think herself very smart but unattractive. Even a boy may think that the only ace he has in his hand is his looks. Otherwise, he's not too smart or talented or able.

Thirteen-year-old Jeremy was a beautiful boy. From the time he was 3 years old, everyone who ran into him would comment to his mother, "Look at those eyes of his. He's gorgeous." However, Jeremy never did well in school. He was a highly creative and intuitive child, but that didn't seem to be translating into the academic arena. In fifth grade it was discovered that he suffered from ADHD. It was also very apparent that he had concluded he wasn't too bright. But, he was good-looking. That he knew.

By the time Jeremy reached seventh grade, he had matured early and turned into a strikingly handsome boy. The girls began chasing him, and he began pivoting in front of the mirror. "Why is my stomach sticking out?

Where's my six pack?" he practically chanted on a regular basis. His mother would consistently try to explain that his body was still changing and that he "was built beautifully" and shouldn't worry.

But Jeremy did worry, and within a two-month period his mother suddenly realized that she could see a rib or two. When she tried to talk it through with her son, all he could say was, "I just don't like feeling fat. I want to look tight. Like I have muscles."

In truth, Jeremy just didn't like feeling stupid at school and was resorting to a kind of obsession with his physical self. It was likely he figured that if he was handsome, he'd better make sure he was as handsome as could be.

Recognizing Inadequacy and Low Self-Esteem
- She constantly compares herself negatively to others.
- Nothing she does ever feels like quite enough to her.
- She's constantly worried that others are mad at her or don't like her.
- She is afraid to try out for any teams or school activity.
- Poor grades convince her that she's stupid.
- She allows others to treat her poorly but insists that they are good friends.

Feelings of Anger

Anger is one of those feelings that many people don't easily tolerate; it is an emotion too powerful, frightening, or overwhelming to contain. And it often signals the underlying presence of depression, loneliness, or inadequacy. At the same time, if it's perceived that there is no way to change what is causing the rage, the feeling can turn into hopelessness, sadness, and the abiding desire to take control of something. In some cases, but by no means is this true across the board, people who suffer with eating disordered behaviors are directing their anger at their bodies instead of those around them.

Carol was caught in a fierce triangle with her parents. Their marriage was a volatile one, with blame being tossed back and forth like a rubber ball and the constant attempt by her mother to drag Carol "into her court." Repeatedly she would make statements to Carol such as "Your father is so selfish," or "He understands nothing," or "I can't stand him one more minute. I just don't know what to do." Carol's father, perceiving the two to be a unit, began to avoid both of them as much as possible.

Carol felt an obligation to soothe her mother and if possible fix things between her parents, but naturally her attempts were fruitless. Carol felt both torn and inadequate. She was also very angry that she was in a war zone and being forced to take a side. The house felt as if it were falling apart, and Carol decided that she would simply have to take care of herself. First thing on the agenda, given the happy lives of all those beautiful movie stars she read about so avidly in the magazines, was to get very thin, too. THAT was sure to improve things. It was her own private plan. It was, in a way, a means to keep a piece of herself away from the household struggle into which she was constantly being pulled.

To Carol, the position she was in was an impossible one, and it was enraging. But there was no room in that house for her anger, so Carol was driven to direct all of those intense feelings into something else—in this case, a diet.

It's also important to note here that "anger" is not always an easy emotion for women. Anger is often perceived as an unattractive, unacceptably unfeminine trait in women. Anger is a man's primal right, but in a woman many still feel that it simply doesn't look good. Girls who embrace the notion that anger isn't "feminine" or desirable in a woman are caught in a trap. They can't simply get rid of the emotion, but they also can't show it. As a result, the conflict is resolved by transforming it into other emotional states that are painful but a disguised expression of their true inner experience. A problem with food begins.

Recognizing Anger
- Signs of depression can sometimes mask anger.

- Ironically, she retains a completely serene manner no matter what is going on, or it takes very little to set her off and she is unable to shake the mood.
- Trouble is erupting in school with reports of rudeness or poor behavior.
- She cries easily over frustration.

Feelings of Loneliness

Loneliness is another of the common feelings among adolescents. A child may feel unable to express herself, be socially immature, feel different from others perhaps because of a problem or tragedy in the family, and assume that no one can understand her. As a result she may keep herself isolated. Sometimes the loneliness is denied or simply unrecognized. Interestingly, however, most adolescents will not define or perhaps even recognize their loneliness as such. They will more often describe themselves as bored instead.

Alexis's parents both worked very hard to support their family and to provide the many things they themselves as children never had. Her mother was somewhat emotionally disconnected from her daughter, as she herself had lost her own mother at a young age. Unable to address her discomfort with the emotional sustenance that she felt she should provide, she allowed herself to view money as her maternal contribution. Alexis was an only child, and though she was repeatedly told how much she was loved, she found herself after school alone every day for hours. She was not a very outgoing girl and had only one or two friends. Alexis at first busied herself by going to their homes for company at least a few times a week, which worked well until Alexis noticed that she was gaining weight. Her friends were not. They also seemed to be getting busier and busier with a new crowd into which Alexis did not feel welcomed. Alexis began to stay home alone and eat. The cookie box had become a kind of pal. Eating had become a comfort.

Then one day she asked to try on a friend's pair of jeans, thinking they looked like a "loose cut." She couldn't zip them and felt humiliated when

*her friend, in an effort to comfort her, said, "Oh, sometimes they don't zip
on me either." That same evening she found out she'd not been invited to
a party that almost everyone in the class was attending. Alexis went
home, threw out the cookies, and skipped dinner altogether. She told her
parents that she wasn't hungry and had eaten before they got home. Alexis
was certain it was the only way not to fall off the social map.*

Loneliness can be experienced as a hollow feeling in the center of
one's being, a hole needing to be filled. And many people, regardless
of age, will symbolically use food to "fill up." The child who, in a
state of painful loneliness, is also experiencing puberty's effect of
putting on weight is vulnerable to flipping a switch—moderation
not being a hallmark of adolescence—turning to dieting as a means
of turning away from what seems too much to bear.

Recognizing Loneliness

Apart from the obvious signs of being isolated and unable to connect with others, your daughter may frequently announce, "There's
nothing to do." "Loneliness" is a word that for many people carries
a kind of shame. Boredom offers the more acceptable possibility—
it's the environment that is faulty. It feels less embarrassing. In truth
this adolescent may feel that there really is nothing to do—except
diet. Ironically, it is the only way she can think of to feel less hungry
for understanding and self-acceptance.

ANXIETY AND ITS RELATED FEATURES

Like depression, the symptoms of anxiety are both physical and
emotional. Witness a person pacing, or sweating, or tossing and
turning, worried that something is about to go terribly wrong. What
if she doesn't do a good enough job or makes a big mistake that cannot be fixed? The physical symptoms can be heart palpitations,

sweaty palms, a tightness in the chest or stomach, and tension-induced headaches. As we get older, most of us learn to take our anxiety and the attendant symptoms as a signal that it's time to find constructive solutions to life's challenges. Most adolescents have yet to develop that skill. They are often hog-tied by their anxieties and stress-inducing experiences and act upon them in ways that don't necessarily scream "I'm anxious!" Anxiety is one of the powerful predisposing factors of eating disorders.

Recognizing Anxiety
- She has heart palpitations, shortness of breath, or a tight feeling in her chest.
- She wakes up repeatedly during the night consumed by worries.
- She has stomachaches.
- She is agitated and restless, always feeling on edge.
- Her mind may frequently go blank.
- Her anxious thoughts frequently get in the way of relaxed socializing.

Extreme Dependence

Many adolescents with fragile self-worth cannot tolerate criticism and incessantly fear negative judgment from others. As a result they constantly aim to please and defer easily to others. It's as if what they think matters little in the face of someone else's opinion. They can have what is known as very dependent personalities.

Maria was the youngest child and only girl in a family of five boys. Her father, an extremely volatile and demanding personality, expected all of his children to participate in athletics. To him it represented discipline, strength, and courage. He wanted his children to have that competitive edge. But Maria was not that sort of personality. Still, both to please him and out of fear, Maria became a volleyball player. She was a good one, but she hated it. She was also furious that her father wouldn't leave her alone. She never felt good enough. Every game she had a stomachache worrying how he'd react if she made a mistake. It was too much, and so Maria made a cognitive switch. A friend had suggested that they go on a low-carb diet together. Maria took that to mean that her friend thought she was fat, and so she started worrying about her figure instead of raging against her father. Her volleyball game improved, and her weight began to drop.

Adolescents who crave approval seek out others for nurturance and to hear constant words of approbation. Unfortunately, they can never quite get enough affirmation. If they don't experience that they are indeed in everyone's good graces, the tension begins to rise and the analgesic aspect of eating disordered behavior can kick in.

Recognizing a Problem with Dependence

- She easily gives in to others.
- She goes to great lengths to get others to like her.
- She is afraid to state her opinion.
- She is decidedly unopinionated, insisting that "It doesn't matter, I'm fine with whatever."

A Need to Be Perfect

This is a personality trait that often arises in families where expectations are high—and where the feature of anxiety is prominent. It can also be self-imposed and is only further enhanced and reinforced by the messages in the media and by peer pressure.

Many adolescents who are struggling with the slippery slope of an eating disorder have imposed very tough standards upon themselves. Whether the pressure originated with the family, from the media, or a healthy dose of both or from within, the drive to be "perfect" can grow intense. It is often a reflection of an adolescent's conviction that she is simply not good enough or loveable unless everything about her is exemplary.

For a girl often driven to exhaustion by this impossible goal, anxiety can enter the picture. On a conscious level, an adolescent may turn this turmoil in on herself, struggling more and more fiercely to get everything right. On an unconscious level, there can also be a slow buildup of anger aimed at parents who are perceived to give their love only if she can objectively be measured as great.

Donna had two highly successful attorney parents who expected nothing less than a superior performance from their daughter. Certainly there were times when they struggled with their own quest for success, and they often tried to tone down their words to Donna, recognizing that they might be too demanding. But Donna wasn't fooled by their seeming acceptance of a B– on a test or a string of losses in tennis competitions. She could sense their frustrations, and hers grew as well—both with herself and with them. Nothing felt as if it was good enough. And so Donna discovered that manipulating her food intake was comforting. She could do that very successfully. At first, since it was so hard to give up delicious foods, she threw up once or twice but couldn't bear the way that felt. And so she began restricting herself, growing prouder each day about her self-control. "I am," she thought, "in charge."

It was only after she was in treatment for about six months that Donna suddenly turned to her mother during a family session and said, with venom in her voice, "If I'd gotten a straight-B report card, I'd have disgusted you." It was the beginning of the expression of her personal truths—the inescapable piece of the puzzle that must emerge before an eating problem can be resolved.

Recognizing a Need to Be Perfect
- She becomes very distressed if anything about her appearance—her outfit, hair, makeup—is not just so.
- She is extremely hard on herself if she makes one or two mistakes on a test.
- She will stay up to all hours of the night getting an assignment "just right."

- She is overly cooperative, rarely causing you to remind her to do *anything*.

SUBSTANCE ABUSE

You've already learned that substance abuse and eating disorders can be closely linked. They each may represent different expressions of the same underlying problem, a predisposition to addictive behavior patterns.

In addition, people who suffer from both substance abuse and an eating disorder tend to maintain the problem behavior despite the negative impacts on their lives. They often deny the severity of the disorder yet experience an accompanying depression. The risk factors for substance abuse and eating disorders can overlap. Just as some girls use food—or the lack of it—to feel comforted and more in control, alcohol and drugs (over-the-counter, prescription, and illegal alike) are similarly employed.

It's important to recognize, however, that alcohol and drugs can also be used by girls to *enable* their dieting. They may take certain over-the-counter drugs to help them lose weight or keep their minds off food. These drugs can suppress weight or initiate a way to purge the body of food. Many girls take more than the recommended daily limit. There are also many herbal and quack pills. Ephedrine, often sold as a Chinese herb, has proven to be extremely dangerous due to heart racing, heart palpations, and death.

Substance abuse, particularly alcohol, is far less common in people suffering from anorexia nervosa than bulimia nervosa. In fact, those girls who are on a slippery slope to anorexia are far less likely to drink or to take illegal drugs than those who are becoming bulimic. Anorexia nervosa is associated with restraint and control, which may protect against the risk of alcohol or drug abuse. Bulimia, however, is often associated with negative emotions and impulsiveness, which may increase a risk of substance abuse.

Many dieters take laxatives or diuretics. You might not think of these as drugs, but just because they aren't illegal doesn't mean they aren't very dangerous. Laxatives cause weight loss through dehydration as a result of watery diarrhea. Unfortunately, few people realize that calorie absorption is not affected by laxative use. The overuse of laxatives can cause acute and chronic lower gastrointestinal complications along with other problems.

Nicotine is also a very popular weight-loss drug. Indeed, studies have shown that nicotine acts much like prescription diet drugs. People keep off five to ten pounds and regain them when they stop smoking. Young people are smoking earlier, and many believe that, in part, this is because of our nation's obsession with staying slim.

Clearly a problem with food is not simply just that. It's the *presenting* problem—the one parents can most readily notice and clearly identify. But it would be a mistake to ever simply try to change the troubling behaviors. It is in fact critical that the adolescent, parents, and professionals look beyond the flirtation with an eating disorder and address the underlying issues that are driving an adolescent's troublesome behaviors. Whether it's depression or anxiety and many or just a few of the attendant unhappy feelings that accompany these diagnoses, you need to help your daughter identify and face what is truly hurting her and then strive to relieve the stressors—whether they are real, imagined, or, as in most cases, both.

The slippery slope to an eating disorder cannot merely be attended to by a vigilant watchfulness at the dinner table, a quiet or loud insistence that "this has to stop," or an eating plan, no matter how well thought-out, that is seemingly easy to adopt and attractively presented.

The question "Why isn't my child eating?" can be answered many different ways. So much depends on what your child brings to the table, so to speak. And therein lies the key. Interestingly, one might say that the best question to ask is, "What is eating up my child?" It's the highly particular answer to that question that will most help you begin to understand what might be done to help your adolescent regain her emotional equilibrium, achieve some measure of body satisfaction, and resume eating healthfully.

In the next three chapters we will take a close look at the three stages of the behavioral slippery slope that could lead to an eating disorder. You may very likely be able to recognize your child at any point on this continuum. But no matter where she is, keep in mind that you can help to effect how and when she gets off that slope and returns to healthy eating. Consider your child's personal world, her social environment, and your family and the child's apparent emotional life and personality traits as you read on. The pieces will start to come together and help you see realistically what is happening and what can be done to turn things around.

five
___

Stage One

The Innocent Dieter

Let us begin by saying that some diets are simply that—finite attempts to lose weight. A target weight is set, your child isn't thinking that it will change her life, and the genuine motivation is to look good. Once this is accomplished, the diet seamlessly melts into a healthy eating pattern.

Still, if you've bought this book, your child has likely dropped a little more weight than you might have preferred. We're going to assume that this child, whom you are worried about, has now expressed in word or deliberate action some significant concern about her weight or body image. If so, it will be hard to know what she's really thinking. The numbers on the scale may be taunting her. The size of certain parts of her body may be of great concern to her. She may not like the way she thinks she is compared to others. Privately she could be thinking, among other things:

"Why do I have to have such fat thighs?"
"My behind is too big for the rest of me."
"How am I going to go to the beach?"

"I am the fattest kid in gym."
"I'm not good enough."

You may or may not understand how she can see herself the way she does. It doesn't really matter. It's what she perceives that matters most.

At this point, your daughter may have stepped onto the slippery slope and has become the innocent dieter. At the very beginning of this stage (which should not imply she necessarily will go any further), it's going to be hard to know whether or not to be concerned. This is so for a few reasons. Perhaps she does need to lose a few pounds. Maybe she doesn't, but you can see the kind of role models she's staring at on TV and can imagine why losing a pound or two might make her feel good. Add to this the fact that it seems as if her eating is relatively normal.

But what is normal in her eyes?

Admittedly, "normal" is different for every child, but there is, generally speaking, a look and feel to healthy eating. The problem is that adolescents who may be edging toward a problem with eating are like magicians. It's hard to tell whether the nibbling, the full plate, and the clattering from the kitchen speak to a normal consumption of food or are really illusions. Is she just munching on celery? Is she actually going to eat everything on the plate? And is the banging around in the kitchen simply a fascination with the cooking of food that she may hardly allow herself to enjoy?

Fortunately at this stage, a diet is easy to see. She's probably talking about it, openly counting calories, munching on carrots, and yet still somewhat regularly consuming a balanced meal. But toward the end of this stage, *if* things continue, you might begin to notice that something different is going on. As time progresses, you may not be sure what or how much she's eating. One minute she might consume a meal before your very eyes. The next, she may leave her plate almost completely full. She still looks healthy. Toward the end of this stage, however, you might begin to notice that there's not much discussion about the diet.

It usually follows that as the talk lessens, so does the weight.

At this point the innocent dieter is likely still displaying some healthy eating habits. But since in the next stage (especially early on) it will be so difficult (if not impossible) to really know if your adolescent is becoming consumed by a diet, it's important that you understand, objectively speaking, what healthy eating looks like. This is not something you want your adolescent to define for you. She'll do so with her magic wand, and you won't know what to think.

Healthy eating and healthy concern about being slim, as described below, have some specific characteristics that should serve as a good baseline for you as you attempt to sort out what, if any, concerns you should have. The innocent dieter, should she decide to extend her weight loss beyond the original goal, may begin in subtle ways to leave healthful eating behind, though she'll undoubtedly claim, "I eat a lot! Don't worry!"

You will need to decide that for yourself.

A Profile on Healthy Eating

- Adolescents who eat normally usually do so at regular times with consistent habits. They're hungry at noon, ready to eat by 7 P.M., and might easily by midafternoon and toward bedtime want a small snack.
- Your child will eat when she is hungry. The statement "I'm starved" ought to be followed up by a flurry of activity in the kitchen as she rummages about for something satisfying. If she's watching her weight, she may choose a carrot, a broiled chicken breast, an apple and low-fat cottage cheese, or a low-fat container of yogurt. These choices are fine as long as they are occasional choices.
- Your child eats in plain sight. She may take an occasional plate up to her room, but she'll settle down at the kitchen table just as easily and talk.
- When she's done, for the most part her plate is empty.

- The amount of food that is eaten at any one time seems reasonable—not so little that it couldn't satisfy a mouse, and not so much as to soothe the hunger pangs of a large animal.
- She makes instinctually natural choices. Most people who are not overly concerned with diet will gravitate over the course of a day or week to all of the five food groups: bread and grains, fruits, vegetables, meat, and milk. It's as if we have an internal monitor that makes sure we get the fifty essential nutrients for growth, energy, and health.

NOTE: Most adolescents do not eat enough fruits or vegetables, nor do they drink enough milk. But this does not herald an eating problem. They just don't enjoy them as much as they used to.

- Your daughter will likely at times talk to you about her diet. She may discuss what she should eat, comment on how she looks, and ask you to buy certain foods. This is a sign that food is just food. She's becoming body-conscious and wants to pay attention to what she's consuming. Exercising restraint with fattening foods is a sign of her healthy desire to control her weight.
- She appears pleased if clothes become looser and she can see that she's dropped some unwanted weight. She steps back and admires herself rather than placing parts of her body under a microscope. She might reward herself with a delicious dessert.
- The ratio of eating to exercising is normal and not even obviously, in her mind, related. She doesn't eat a full meal and then run for three miles. She runs two miles with her track team every other day and then eats because she's hungry.
- She visits the bathroom scale once a day, randomly if that, instead of after every meal.
- She eats socially. It's a pleasurable activity.
- After she eats she feels good, satisfied.

The Subtleties of the Innocent Diet

The innocent dieter could be any teen. She might be slightly over-weight or involved in a sport that would seem to require her to slim down. She might live in a family where fitness is a priority, or she might feel unpopular and think that maybe if she was thinner more people would like her. The innocent dieter might simply want to diet to join her friends or fit into a particularly great pair of jeans, which she bought just a bit too tight. She might have gotten her period earlier than her friends and be self-conscious about the resulting curves ("fat").

The point is, it is certain that at first she has no intention of becoming *too* thin—just thin enough to feel good. Her self-image and level of concern about her weight may be uneven. Still, there are signs of a subtle internal struggle.

At the beginning she will likely be quite the talker but an inter-mittent dieter. This means she may openly state that she feels too heavy and appear determined to lose weight, but she goes about doing so in a haphazard way. One day she may skip a meal, the next day not. This might cause her to be annoyed at herself. She may try eating celery sticks for lunch a few days in a row and then in the midst of a busy day with friends eat a hamburger and fries without a second thought, until she gets home. She may look in the mirror and readily be able to identify what she doesn't like but still not quite be ready to do anything serious about it. Her body image might be low, but the motivation to do something about it seesaws.

What follows are three different profiles of girls facing different life issues. Along the way we'll point out the possible signs of con-cern you should notice and then offer suggestions for what you can do. Some of these suggestions will be interchangeable between pro-files, while some are specific to the challenges each girl faces. Taken as a whole, however, they will offer a useful map for what to do and what to say when you notice that your daughter is showing concern for her weight.

An Innocent Dieter: To Keep a Guy

Fourteen-year-old Lisa had always been a very pretty girl with a beautiful face and a lovely shape. Her parents were divorced when she was quite young, and years later her mother remarried a very formal, somewhat rigid man who while not unfair was a far cry from the easygoing father Lisa could remember. Her father had moved clear across the country, and although she saw him once a year, it never felt like enough.

Around age 14 Lisa, a bit prematurely for her emotional abilities, began a relationship with Donovan who was one year older. He was quite handsome and flirted a good deal with other girls. Lisa was afraid she would lose him and began worrying every day. Her friends told her not to worry, but Lisa repeatedly asked, "Am I pretty? Am I fat? Maybe he doesn't think I'm good-looking enough." Her friends were unanimous in their support, but Lisa felt that the mirror said something different.

One day she tried skipping breakfast and lunch but got so hungry that she almost fainted walking home, so she shot into the local deli with a friend and gobbled an ice cream cone. That felt good.

But the next day, Lisa got up extra early to stand to the side and survey her stomach. It seemed a bit round. Then again, she was hungry. She walked downstairs and encountered her mother in the kitchen.

"Mom," Lisa asked, "do you think I'm a little overweight?"

"Not at all," came the reply, surprise evident in her mother's voice.

"I think I'd like to lose around five pounds," Lisa said. She began reading the labels on the sides of the cereal boxes and, shaking her head, put them back in the cupboard.

"Sounds like a lot," her mom answered, somewhat absentmindedly checking her palm pilot to figure out what time she needed to be in the office. "Eat an apple if you're worried," she added as she kissed her daughter goodbye.

Lisa grabbed a granny smith from the refrigerator.

Yes. She was worried. Probably her mother was too. Otherwise she wouldn't have mentioned the stupid apple.

Still, that afternoon, she ate a serving of french fries and ketchup.
That is, until she saw Donovan enter the cafeteria. Then she stopped.
What, after all, would he think?

Lisa wants to lose weight, but her whole self isn't in it yet. Part of her knows she looks good, but there's another voice that speaks to a shaky sense of her own self-worth and is heightening the expectations she has of herself. She's still eating because everyone around her is, and it's hard to control her appetite under those circumstances. Everything smells so good. Of course, Donovan is a problem. She'd caught him admiring a picture of a beautiful actress in a bikini the other day when he was flipping through a magazine. Lisa had leaned over his shoulder and frowned. It was possible, though doubtful, that she could get *that* thin.

Lisa is getting it from all sides. While her family is not of the chaotic type, as described in chapter 3, there has been some unhappy reorganization of key family members. Her past is one in which she might have felt abandoned by her father—to say the least. Presently she is quite resentful of her stepfather, who from her perspective always has to have things "just so." Low self-esteem (at least in part a result of being "left" by her father) and feeling disregarded at home (at least in part due to the rigid rules) could at this point be significant problems for her. Lisa has a popular boyfriend, and as she well knows in her school thin is in and fat is out, and anyone overweight does *not* attract boys. Donovan, she thinks, could move on at any time. And then there's her digitally improved glossy magazine competition. What was she supposed to do about that?

This could be the point of departure for most girls who are about to step onto the slippery slope of dieting that may or may not lead to more serious eating problems. Unfortunately, it's hardly visible. You'd have to be looking, and you'd have to be able to read Lisa's thoughts to predict her next move. But Lisa's mother still has information that should help her keep her eyes and ears open. What does she know?

- Her daughter has suffered the kind of loss that might have left her feeling very unimportant.
- She is in a newly created family in which the person who rules the roost is difficult for her to connect with. It's his rules, almost all the time.
- She has asked if she's fat.
- She's studying food labels.
- She clearly has no idea that five pounds is quite a bit of weight.

At this point, is there anything her mother can do? Realistically, there may not be much. She's not aware of her daughter's insecurity with Donovan—in fact she hardly knows who he is. She might have gotten her daughter into counseling because of the problems at home, but Lisa seemed okay, and so it hasn't seemed necessary. And besides, girls worrying about their weight is as common as rain.

In Response You Can
- In order to glean some idea of the source, ask why your daughter feels fat. NOTE: *Do not* tell her "You don't need to lose weight." Not only does she not agree with you, but she will think you haven't a clue about how she feels. Instead say something like "What is it that is making you think you need to lose weight? This is something we need to talk about."
- No matter how she replies, don't argue. Remarks such as "Oh, don't be ridiculous" won't fly. However, saying something like "Well, I can't say I agree with you, but if you really want to lose a few pounds, let's talk about a healthy way to do it." This will communicate that you are on her side.
- During a quiet moment when you notice your child pondering the food in a cupboard, say something like "Those labels can be misleading. Want me to go through them with you?" Then explain what food labels mean including such topics as

how many carbs are too many, what is saturated fat, and more. If you don't know, read up on the issues (see the "Further Reading" list).

- The next time your adolescent mentions being fat, show her a chart, which you've kept on hand for the right moment, that indicates normal weights for girls of different builds, and explore where your child thinks she fits in (see the BMI charts in the appendix). Help her evaluate whether or not she is accurate. "What makes you think you're small-boned?" "What do you mean you think you are 'thick'?" (This is a word lots of girls use to describe muscle that deep down they think is fat.) Be prepared, however, for your daughter to scoff at the chart. She may say, "What's that got to do with me? Most of these numbers are based on fat people." And in a way she's right. The charts *are* based on average Americans who do tend to be heavier than adolescents would like to be at any height. However, this doesn't mean she won't tuck away the information that in fact she's not so overweight according to some (invisible) authority.

- As hard as it might be to admit, try to identify a family dynamics problem that might be upsetting to your daughter and invite her to talk about it. Whether she can open up or not, comment that you are going to try to improve things. "I know Dad can seem not to listen when you're talking. It isn't a good thing. I'm going to talk to him." Children who are not left alone to "manage" their difficult feelings are less likely to turn inward in search of self-comforting (but destructive) behaviors.

- If perchance you actually agree that a loss of five pounds might look good on her, *keep it to yourself!* Encouragement of any kind, even if specifically stated such as "I think five pounds is an okay idea, but no more," will be heard, by a vulnerable adolescent, as nothing short of "You look fat to me."

The Innocent Dieter: A Quiet Loser

The innocent dieter may have been quite upset by the addition of the pounds that accompanied puberty. She may still be carrying around some "baby fat." The loss of a few pounds might indeed be a good thing. She might begin by deciding that it's time to skip a meal every day or start researching various diets. She might consult with friends, get on the web and look around for the most promising plan, or simply and fairly sensibly start cutting out calories.

This is fine. After a few weeks she might reach her goal of losing ten pounds, look in the mirror, and think, "I look pretty good!" She might then allow herself a scoop of ice cream to celebrate.

This girl has a view of herself that remains clear. She reached her goal, and that's enough.

Unfortunately, many innocent dieters have a way of slipping past this place, discovering that the ten pounds isn't quite good enough. Perhaps she can look better. She's not starving herself by any means, but she is cutting back—and liking it.

Kathy had always been just a few pounds overweight. She passed through puberty quickly and ended up with a curvaceous figure. In fact, sometimes it embarrassed her. She just wanted to be like everyone else. So for a while, to comfort herself, Kathy ate. She didn't like the way boys looked at her breasts, so she wore big clothes. Disappearing into the scene felt safer. She never let it get out of hand, however, and if society's expectations had not been what they are, she might have been considered just a little above average. Kathy began to keep to herself more, as her feelings of inhibition were sometimes overwhelming.

At age 17 Kathy decided that it was time to lose weight. She didn't discuss it with her mother. She could have, but she didn't think it was necessary. After all, her grades were good, she was a gifted art student, and mostly she'd experienced her parents as being very proud of her. They had high expectations of all three children in the family, and no one disappointed. They hardly ever argued. Disagreements were handled, but quietly. High-pitched arguments in this family were unheard of.

So Kathy quietly dieted. No one at home seemed to notice that she skipped all snacks and desserts. She set a goal of ten pounds. It would get her down to 110.

But when Kathy reached 110, it still seemed to her that her hips were not quite right, and so her goal changed to 105.

Kathy's mother noticed right about then and stepped in with characteristic contained concern. "You're getting rather thin," she informed her daughter. "Do you feel okay?"

Kathy didn't know what to say. She didn't feel too thin. She didn't feel fat either. What she did feel was good and completely uninterested in anyone getting in the way.

She shrugged. "I'm fine," she replied, hoping that would be that.

"You have to eat a full dinner tonight," her mother insisted gently.

Kathy nodded.

That evening at the table she ate a small chicken breast, some asparagus, and one new potato. She politely turned down dessert. Then she excused herself from the table.

Kathy's parents weren't sure what was going on but couldn't think of a thing to say.

Kathy went upstairs and began to wonder if jumping rope one hundred times would make up for the potato.

Kathy is starting to hone her magician skills. She's eating, but she's getting a little too thin. This family has aspects of the emotionally inhibited and high-expectation families. They do not as a matter of course emotionally dive in when there's a problem. They hang back, expect success, and when a problem does assert itself they *will* talk. Quietly. But it has to be a big problem. Otherwise they go with the flow. They're not a wholly unhealthy family. They're just reserved and, perhaps because of the way these parents grew up, repressed. Perhaps in their childhood homes big emotional displays were frowned upon. They are, however, quite goal-oriented. They expect a lot from their children. In turn, Kathy expects a lot from herself—in all ways.

Kathy's mother unfortunately knows too little about her children's emotional life. But if she cared to look, she would see that

- From the moment Kathy got her period she began hiding her body behind big clothes.
- Her daughter had been putting on weight and was less social than she had been in younger years.
- Kathy had begun to lose weight without a single comment from anyone in the family. Not even a "good for you."

Kathy's parents don't like conflict and give each other lots of space for privacy. Not too many questions are asked. As a result, nothing much is shared. And also as a result, Kathy has moved ahead with her plan without interference. It is not, however, too late to turn things around.

In Response You Can
- Communicate that a diet is something with a beginning, a middle, and an end. It's not a way of life. Help her talk about her goals. While watching her select a carrot for a snack you might try saying, "That's healthy and low in calories. Not a bad choice. What's the goal?"
- Reflect honestly on your family style. "You know we're not a family that talks about tough subjects very much. I know that. But I'm worrying about you. I see you're dieting, and I want to make sure you're taking care of yourself."
- Though you might be a family that stays away from more delicate personal subjects, your child might need to hear that she can talk about her body. She may need an opening. "You know, I've noticed you are losing weight and you look good—but I wouldn't like to see you get much thinner. How do you feel about the way you look now?" If she says "Fine" and offers nothing else, try some straight talk to indicate that you're not embarrassed. "You're very curvy. Some kids would love that. Do you?"
- Be positive and complimentary. "You know you look great to me. I'm wondering why you feel you need to diet. I'd love to understand how you see yourself."

- Ask her how she *feels*. "Do you feel happy at this weight?" "I'm wondering if you don't feel a little tired or hungry."
- Offer help that expresses understanding and interest. "Can I help you plan a healthy diet—I know you want to be thin, and I promise we'll do it carefully. What's a comfortable way for you?"
- If you're a family of high expectations, own up to it and make it clear that she's more important than the high standard. Don't say that she doesn't have to meet your standards, because she may feel that you think she can't. But you can say, "Look, I know I make a big deal about a straight-A report card. That's because I know you're capable. But you're just as smart if you get a B here and there, and you'll probably be a lot happier. That's important to me. Stress is a bad thing." In Kathy's case, it might be comforting for her to know that someone knows behind the straight A's is a very anxious child.

Sometimes, especially with a child who isn't talking much, it's important to stay away from questions and instead make exploratory statements. "I'm wondering if you feel worried that I'll be angry if you don't do well on that test." "I can see you are interested in losing weight. I'm hoping you aren't being too strict about it. You look good to me."

Adolescents frequently feel as if they are being "pumped" for info. Speaking with statements is a softer, less confrontational approach and one that works well in families where confrontation does not come easy.

Innocent Dieter: Thin Is the #1 Goal

Other innocent dieters may want to diet because there's an emphasis in the house on physical fitness, because someone continually teases them in school as if their weight is the only thing that counts, because their friends are doing it, or because quite simply they can diet and it feels good.

Ellie's father was and always had been obsessive about orderliness, exercising, and weight. He regularly hauled his kids off to the gym to exercise right along with him. This started when Ellie was around 12 years old. At first she hated the routine.

Ellie was a good athlete and had always been proud of her strength and agility. She competed in volleyball and tennis, and she excelled in both. At around age 14 Ellie discovered boys, and they discovered her. Suddenly she was dabbling in makeup, insisting on a new haircut every few months, and constantly begging for new clothes that seemed more and more revealing. She also started reading packaging labels and purchasing her own foods. They were all "lite" or "diet" or "fat free." Ellie's mother didn't like this at all, but Ellie looked just great and so her mother wasn't sure what to do. She did buy French vanilla ice cream and put it in the freezer, knowing it was Ellie's favorite, but it remained untouched. Even Ellie's friends seemed to be dropping weight.

Soon she began to notice that Ellie was eating not one other thing from the kitchen cabinet but diet foods. She didn't know what to do. Or think. Ellie did look good. Thin though.

Even if her mother was confused, Ellie knew precisely what she was doing, and it was getting to be fun.

She didn't exactly enjoy the gym with her dad, but it felt satisfying— as if she was really accomplishing something important. Every few days the numbers on the scale were moving downward. She was almost at her goal—whatever that was. Ellie figured she'd know it when she saw it.

Ellie's mom is confused because her daughter still looks good. She's a busy working mother with so much "on her plate" that she isn't fully noticing what's not on her daughter's. Despite Ellie's father's abundant interest in keeping things under control, that in itself can create chaos within the family. The children are in a bind. They are, indirectly, being asked to become obsessive, which is likely quite uncomfortable for them. Yet to argue could create unwanted conflict. Conceivably Ellie might decide, unconsciously, that it's easier to join her father than to fight him. After all, it fits with the social demands of her circle anyway. These dynamics go on silently, of course. But still, what her mother can likely see is that

- Her daughter is concentrating on diet foods.
- She had always thought her husband obsessive about his body, but she'd assumed she would be the role model for her daughter. She needs to realize that children can choose to emulate the traits of the opposite-sex parent as well.
- Sometimes children can simply inherit a potentiality for traits. Genetics can play a role in the vulnerability toward an eating disorder just as compulsive traits can run in families. It can show up at first in a certain rigidity—for example, only diet foods. Then as time goes on the obsessiveness can deepen and impinge on everything from grooming to schoolwork to sports. A child has to be helped to loosen up and see that flexibility will not lead to disaster.
- She could do some research and find out that obsessiveness can be a genetic trait.
- Her daughter may be trying to please the father with whom she spends less time.

In Response You Can
- Ask what kind of diet a child is on and offer some suggestions in accordance to what's important to the specific child. Ellie, for instance, might be interested in counting carbs or calories or both. Talk with her about what's a healthy amount of both with a noncomplex book on hand that she might want to scan (see the "Further Reading" list).
- If you suspect that she's obsessed with boys and the way in which they see her, ask what qualities she thinks they look for in a girl. If she proceeds with a litany of perfect body parts,

listen until she is through. Then nod sympathetically and say, "I can see what worries you, but is that what you would like a person for? What about his brains? His sense of humor? You love to laugh!" She may roll her eyes, but say it anyway.

- If you have the time, peruse the teen magazines and see if you can find an article written from a sensitive perspective that speaks to what a boy looks for in a girl. Sometimes a piece entitled something like "What a Boy Secretly Looks for in A Girl" reveals male vulnerabilities that might surprise your daughter. Of course, read the article first!

- Try to find out when your daughter intends to stop dieting. What's her goal weight? If it seems low, drag out the tables to show her why you think so.

- Talk about what obsessive behaviors can look like and how much they can get in the way of someone's life. A little education will not give her "ideas" or worsen her already troublesome behavior. Defining obsessive behaviors might, in fact, help her become more aware and in control of her rigid demands upon herself. Don't be afraid to say that you worry about the way her father (or anyone she cares for) obsesses about things. "I know Dad is a little fanatical about being thin, but frankly I think it's unhealthy, and honestly I don't think he much enjoys it."

- Ask her why her friends like to diet, too, and whether or not they tend to compare weight. Tell her that's kind of like hoping they each wear the same shoe size! "You can squeeze your feet into the same shoe, but it's going to be a terrible fit because people's feet are built differently." Point out, however, that if they all buy the right size, they'll look and feel great.

So far these girls simply fall into the category of needing to have their dieting behaviors recognized. It's unclear where they are going. Questions abound. When will they stop? What are they feeling like now? Will they get bored? Hungry? Is this just a group activity? Are her friends doing the same thing? Perhaps she's just frightened. As she becomes less afraid of growing up, she might relax her eating habits. No parent can know the answers for sure.

At the innocent dieter stage, the unfortunate truth is that there's really only one way to know when there might eventually be a significant problem: the dieting doesn't stop.

At the more benign end of the spectrum, the dieting might persist because of the compliments received. There is something extremely intoxicating about peers sayings, "Wow, you look great!" "You got so thin! I'm so jealous!" "Those jeans look so good on you!" Although it can become addictive, an adolescent might simply bask in the admiration for a short while and then determine that she's reached her goal. On the other hand, if a problem is building her thoughts might go to, "Well, if they think I look good now, just wait until I lose a little more."

At this more toxic end of the reasoning spectrum, the adolescent is finding that the control she has over her body is beginning to make her feel powerful. Finally, there is a way for all those nagging feelings of insecurity, unexpressed anger, or depression to express themselves and be relieved. She's beginning to feel in control. And those compliments! Ultimately, it feels as if everything is coming together.

Well, of course it isn't. In fact, innocent dieters who keep thinking "maybe just one more pound" are at the place where things are just beginning to take a difficult turn. "If she could just stop now," many parents think, showering their child with such statements as "Enough! You're perfect!" or "You look so good right now. Stop worrying. Eat!" But many innocent dieters and probably most of the adolescents in the next two stages suffer from an interesting inability to conceive of one thing: the principle of maintenance. They understand dieting and not dieting, but the area in between is simply nonexistent.

Explaining the Concept of Maintenance

Most adolescents, putting all reason aside, are afraid that if they go off their diets and start eating more, no matter how carefully, they will begin to put weight back on. The idea that this may not be so or that a weight fluctuation of a pound or two makes no difference in appearance seems impossible. Nonsensical really. It's just an adult's plan to make them gain weight. Even the adolescent who is in possession of diet books, almost all of which contain chapters on maintenance, seem to view those pages as being about as important as an index.

So, urge your daughter to read those pages. If she doesn't, read the chapter yourself and during a discussion, in snippets (lectures are despised), offer up the key information.

An adolescent who is hungry and simply likes being thin because she just enjoys the way she looks will ultimately explore the idea of being satisfied with her weight and dare to step outside the boundaries she has set for herself. After all, she does miss her banana ice cream. If the diet is not a form of self-comfort, going off it will not be a danger to her emotional state. The teen who is finding emotional release from the weight loss may not. Maintenance for her may be nothing more than a word that stands in the way of her increasing relief and happiness. And that is simply not acceptable.

If your adolescent is still unsure, suggest that she experiment for two weeks and see what happens. If she doesn't buy that, then try one week. But plan for success. Work out an eating plan that will keep her weight almost exactly as is.

The idea of experimenting, however, may not work with all adolescents, as some young dieters feel that once they let go of the strict regiment they've gone on, it will all come apart. They'll lose control, gain weight, and be unable to stop that gain. In a later stage you will find that this thinking is somewhat based on fact. When the body is seriously starved, the child might indeed begin bingeing, unable to reintroduce moderation without professional help.

This is not where your child is right now, though hunger pangs will inspire her to consider her options. The innocent dieter may allow some sweets here and there, but she will be watching like a hawk to see how her body responds.

Maintenance simply seems to be a concept many kids cannot comfortably embrace.

The innocent dieter needs to be watched. She needs to be spoken and listened to. She needs to know that you are on her side, that you understand she wants to be thin. If you sense other things might be bothering her, say so. Let her know that you genuinely care about who she is and not just what she can accomplish. And most importantly, she needs to get the message from you, repeatedly, that thin is nice but that her humor, her intelligence, her compassion for others, and her determination are all qualities you admire about her. If these qualities result in popularity, great grades, or winning the class presidency, that is good, but what matters most is that she like and enjoy herself.

Finally, listen to the messages beneath your words, before you speak them.

You might be tempted to say, "You are the best player on your tennis team." But try, "You play a terrific game." The first statement says that what counts is that you're the best. The child walks away thinking, I'd better keep it up. The second statement says, what you did was wonderful. The child walks away feeling proud of her level of skill without comparing herself to others.

You might be tempted to say as your daughter walks out the door, "Honey, comb your hair. And please tuck your shirt in. People will think you're so sloppy!" But consider this. If the goal is to help your child not be so concerned with how others view her body, won't this sort of statement negate that goal? It's critical to bring her to a place where what matters is how *she* feels the happiest. "I guess you're going for the relaxed look today" communicates that you think she's a bit rough about the edges but also lets her know that how she wants to look is up to her, and *ought* to be up to her. The truth is that if every adolescent girl bought that idea, there might be fewer dieters.

You have a chance in this stage to nudge your child back to a place where being thin is one of many goals. Where it is a wish, not a mission. An ideal she may give some thought to each day, but one that can easily fade into the shuffle of a daily happy, productive life in which being thin is *not* the ultimate prize.

six

Stage Two

The Exhilarated Dieter

The move from innocent dieting to the exhilarated stage is very subtle. It represents a quiet shift in daily focus of which even the dieter may sometimes only be slightly aware. One hallmark of the shift, however, is that while before she may have spent a fair amount of time worrying about her weight, she was also still worried about her grades, obsessing about which boy had stared at her the longest, or whether or not her best friend is really just that. Now she has a new and slowly growing, singular obsession: weight loss. And it's a thrill. Unlike worrying about what boy likes what girl or how she could squeeze in an hour of studying for the science quiz and still go out after school for a soda, a new activity is beginning to take center stage: planning her menu. It's simple, it's controllable, and it's all hers.

It isn't that school doesn't matter, or that she won't make it to *every* volleyball practice, or that Peter smiling at her doesn't make her day. It's that menu and food control are new, happy companions.

Jill watched with irritation as her best friend Melinda pulled out her calorie counter and started planning the next day's menu. She'd been trying to get Melinda interested in the argument she'd just had with another friend.

117

"You're not listening to me," Jill snapped. "I am," Melinda replied, shaking her head vigorously. "Kate told you that she thinks you're selfish, and Robert laughed when you got upset." Jill shrugged her shoulders. That was about it. But somehow Melinda looked so preoccupied. She watched as her friend started jotting down fat grams. "Ya know," Jill sighed, "It's like you have a new best friend. Your stupid diet."

Melinda looked up, bewildered. "What are you talking about?"

Jill just stared at her. It was just a feeling. Way too hard to explain.

The exhilaration of dieting is a seductive feeling. It's filled with so much promise. Certainly not every girl who falls into this category feels nothing but elation, as we shall soon see, but she is counting on the real and anticipated future success to finally make her feel complete.

So, what is the exhilarated dieter thinking? Essentially, she's thinking that she is going to enjoy a big success. This may be true for some, but others cannot know at this point that there is a potential danger ahead: that she can never succeed, that whatever weight she achieves will never be good enough. For now, she has set out to perfect her figure, and she is doing it.

Typically, at this point she is likely thinking that

- My body can and will be just what I've always wanted!
- I've succeeded so well at something others only talk about.
- I'm going to reap the benefits of a beautiful body—more friends, romance, looks of admiration.
- The dieting really makes me feel so great! Energized! Happy!
- Things will finally be exactly right.
- Everyone keeps saying that I look so good! What a kick!

The exhilarated dieter is becoming engrossed, caught up with the pleasure of becoming thin. It isn't a thought that's with her every moment of the day, but she is definitely feeling a kind of high—a sense of glorious well-being. She is doing the right thing.

She is on the good path. Nothing can stop her now. And if there have been problems in her life she couldn't fix, well, now it hardly matters because now *she* is in control.

Again, not every girl remains simply exhilarated—utterly convinced that now everything in her world will fall into place. There are those who are vaguely aware that things still aren't good enough, and even those who are cognizant that the exhilaration helps them cope with the pain of certain situations that thinness doesn't seem to fix.

But always there is the dream that, in the end, the ideal weight will bring the ideal life. Whatever either of those things are.

WHAT THE EXHILARATED DIETER MAY "LOOK" LIKE

Generally speaking the exhilarated dieter is far more self-satisfied than she's ever been, and at times even excited. The world is about to become her oyster. Maybe.

This seemingly confident girl who is manifesting a very stringent attitude toward food at this stage looks thinner than she had been, but not alarmingly so. She feels wonderful that all of her friends are complimenting her and mostly quite disdainful that her parents may be voicing concerns. "You just don't get it," she replies. "This is the way I want to look. *Everyone* loves it."

She has not dropped any balls, either. While the "star" of the show may be serious dieting, she is still interested in staying on top in every other way. She works hard; she's feeling even more competitive; her optimism is starting to soar; and she's *very* busy both internally and externally. She may be racing around from track meet to track meet, dragging her books to be sure of an A, and practicing with the school band with a renewed intensity. But much of the apparent energy is not, as it had been before, being fueled by the everyday successes she works so hard to achieve. The energy source is beginning to be the exhilaration of weight loss. "Getting thin" is not yet a panacea for everything, but it's an ever-present positive force.

The exhilarated dieter is feeling more and more in control of who she is. She's figured out that if she plans carefully and deviates hardly at all, she can grow thinner. Like the innocent dieter, she may request fat-free foods, lessen her food portions, grow critical of the way you cook, and skip dessert altogether. Unlike the innocent dieter, she may occasionally ask to eat in a secretive manner ("I have a big test to study for. Can I eat in my room tonight?"), play ambivalently with her food (she eats most of her steak but does so reluctantly), and exaggerates what she has consumed ("I just ate half a pizza!") just to make sure you leave her alone. But the greatest difference between the exhilarated dieter and the innocent dieter is how they each incorporate their eating habits into their lives. The innocent dieter may clearly display some amount of devotion to her diet. But the innocent dieter has lots of other things on her mind. However, the exhilarated dieter's mind is beginning to lose its clutter as it becomes more involved with a seemingly simple straightforward job: losing weight.

Like the girl at the end of stage one, the exhilarated dieter doesn't know how much she wants to lose. She figures she'll know it when she sees it. The problem is, of course, that maybe she will and maybe she won't.

As the parent you may have a different but related problem that merits some attention here. It's the "now you see it, now you don't" syndrome. An adolescent who has entered the exhilaration stage may appear one day to be heading for trouble and the next return to a basically normal eating pattern. What then?

IS SHE, OR ISN'T SHE?

You may not be able to clearly know if your child is heading for serious trouble at this point on the slippery slope. This is for two reasons:

1. She may spend a few days eating in obvious restrictive ways, and then suddenly you'll find her eating a healthy, well-planned meal.
2. She may in fact eat in very restrictive ways, but at the point at which she approaches the final stage of the slippery slope before an eating disorder (see chapter 7), she may decide that she's had enough. She's fine. She looks thin. Time to party.

There is no easy answer to this dilemma. We cannot tell you to sit back and relax, that the truth will come out. You will want to stay vigilant, but you will also need to *curb* your desire to say, "What are you doing to yourself?" You know what she's doing. She's dieting perhaps a little too excessively, and at this point you are keeping watch to see how far she's going to go with it. Is it getting extreme or isn't it?

Here is a list of things you might say and do during this time to satisfy *your* need to maintain a presence in your daughter's possible problem, and help her feel successful and able to maintain some balance about her self-image. You will want her to see that you are there for her, not to fight with her.

- Address the weight loss in a positive but not overly enthusiastic way. "You have certainly lost weight, honey. You're looking good." In this way you'll be helping her to feel successful but also transmitting that losing weight is not tantamount to a Nobel Prize.
- Discuss the issue of maintenance. Some exhilarated dieters know when to stop. Other's don't. Or can't. They are too afraid of getting "fat" again or feeling terrible about themselves (or circumstances) once more. It isn't necessarily that they want to get skinnier. They simply don't know how to stay where they are. You might want to suggest a nutritionist by saying something like "I can see you want to stay just

where you are. That can be tricky. How about I take you to someone who can help you maintain your weight so that you *can* eat and still feel great?"

- If you are aware that there have been difficult circumstances in her life, you might reasonably assume that they are at least in part behind her current exhilarated dieting. It is possible that she has "swallowed" her emotional pain only to express it through a form of dieting that causes her both discomfort (hunger) and a seemingly wonderful sense of well-being. She feels great! Before she was dragging, but now there seems to be a way out. Whether or not you are clear about her dieting, you might want to suggest a therapist. We talk about this in chapter 8, but for now, suffice it to say that if you sense she has not allowed herself to express the inevitable difficult emotions some circumstances can inspire, they are likely festering somewhere. The dieting may be a way for her to hide from them. If she insists that she doesn't need to talk to a professional, try suggesting that *you* need to because you are concerned about the pressure she's been under and would like to talk with her and a therapist to make sure she's getting what she needs so *you* can relax.

Now let's look at three different exhilarated dieter's experiences and what you as a parent might do in the face of your child's growing sense of accomplishment and increasing weight loss.

EXHILARATION WITHIN REASON

Tori had never concerned herself much with her weight until she reached the age of 16. Then she began dieting. Her diet lasted for nearly a year and decreased her weight from 126 to 106 pounds. She maintained this weight for months. She was 5'1". Her self-discipline at first was almost a wonder to behold. "You are so dedicated," her mother, something of a perfectionist, would initially comment, pride clearly evident. But this observation began to slowly melt into a quiet concern. Tori would not back off from her steadfast commitment to avoid foods rich in calories and fat, and her weight again slowly began to drop.

Around the time Tori's weight reached 101 her mother decided to have her daughter checked by the pediatrician, who rather bluntly announced that she may be developing an eating disorder. This was said despite the fact that Tori had included in her diet healthful foods such as fresh vegetables, chicken breasts, fish, and oranges (a fruit she could not resist).

Tori balked at the doctor's proclamation, thinking her weight ideal, but was next marched off to a nutritionist who spent a few sessions educating an annoyed but somewhat available Tori as to the basics of a healthful meal plan. Tori added low-fat yogurt every other day or so. The nutritionist seemed optimistic that while Tori's idea of an ideal weight was lower than any of the adults in her life would have liked, she was not obsessing about food every minute of the day, exercised only briefly each morning, never induced vomiting, and thought diet pills something of a fake way to achieve her goal. In fact Tori was quite happy with her new appearance and enjoyed the attention she was now receiving from boys, her new wardrobe of form-fitting clothes, and the endless flattery from her friends who were equally caught up in society's concept of the perfect body. Today, Tori likes what she sees on the scale though often complains that "my weight never stays exactly the same."

Is Tori okay? At this point there is no reason to assume otherwise. She has not turned her entire self over to the pursuit of thinness. She's still on the soccer team. She enjoys practicing the flute. She likes a good novel and enjoys all the same friends.

Sure, she's staring in the mirror a lot. But girls her age are naturally extremely concerned with their looks. She seems to be getting a big bang out of turning from what might have been a robust swan into a graceful, slim version of her former self. She's getting the attention she (and most girls her age) want.

And most importantly, she's dancing around a weight of 103 pounds. Maybe one pound up, and one pound down. It's thin to be sure. But at 5'1" it's not dangerous. It's simply worth watching.

Well, you might ask, if I have to watch it, isn't it a problem? The answer is simply that as conscientious parents you will want to keep an eye on any future developments. If your child comes home from a party where there has likely been some drinking but she herself has sweet breath and is clearly in control of all her senses, you will heave a sigh of relief. But are you going to assume that this is the way she'll return home each Saturday night? Certainly not. She might, but you can't take that chance.

And so it is with intense dieting. At this time, Tori's dieting is not chaotic, secretive, or even dangerously lacking in necessary nutrition. Still, despite the lack of any imminent danger, Tori's mother should take note of these facts:

- Tori is thrilled to be thin and basks in the compliments, showing signs of being unsure when to quit.
- She seems to enjoy planning her meals, strictly controlling her food intake, and shows no signs of saying "Okay. I've had enough. Take me to the nearest milk shake."
- She frequently comments that she needs new jeans or shorts—an indication that her clothes are no longer fitting. She may couch these requests with "I need something cool," especially if you've commented a bit too often on her weight loss.
- Tori comes from a family of "strivers." The expectation is that everyone will do their very best at whatever they undertake.

Tori is an exhilarated dieter who seems to have a realistic view of herself. She would appear to have had an endgame and is sticking to it. She feels great. Tori is the least worrisome of the stage two dieters because her foot isn't on the gas and she seems self-satisfied. The problem is, of course, that she might decide either because of a stressful situation or a careless comment that in fact she hasn't quite got it right. This is where her parents come in.

In Response You Can

- It appears that the best approach you can take when you notice your child carefully watching her food intake, losing weight, and clearly enjoying the outcome is to join her "team" as the voice of reason. What you don't want is your child to see you as someone who would stand in the way of her "most excellent adventure." However, what you do want to convey is that as a member of her team you are going to be watching her. You do not intend to look away and simply let her travel down a path that could hurt her health.

- Tell her that you admire the way she's stuck to her diet, but you are also wondering if she has a goal. Lots of adolescents become so excited about their weight loss that they can make the subtle cognitive move from "If I could just reach 102 pounds" to "Wow, I could just keep doing this until I'm REALLY thin" within a blink of an eye. Speaking of a goal may help to remind her that healthy weight loss is not an open-ended endeavor.

- If your child insists that her friends tell her she looks great, agree with them—to a point. Let her know that you under-stand why she's enjoying the way her clothes feel. "Yes, you do look very good. Your clothes look great, though I always thought you looked terrific in your old jeans, too."

- Remind your child, as she is expressing how good she feels about the way she looks, that there are other things to admire about herself as well. "You know, you are wonderful inside, too. Let me tell you the things that I really admire in you." Then list them.

- Express your concerns through the concept of maintenance. In other words, you are not asking her to put on weight. You are, however, clearly saying that from your perspective she's as thin as she can be without things becoming bad for her health. "Frankly, honey, I think at this point that we need to talk about ways to keep you at this weight. You are quite thin. I understand you feel proud of that. But any more weight loss and it could affect your health."

THE EXHILARATION OF FEELING ALL IS RIGHT WITH THE WORLD AND IT CAN ONLY GET BETTER

Dina started worrying about her weight around age 14. At about the same time, her mother suffered a minor heart attack.

Dina had always considered herself to be saddled with some "leftover baby fat," but it hadn't bothered her much until her mother's health faltered. She'd felt she was about normal weight, she fit in with her friends, and she wasn't even particularly concerned about attracting boys. She'd enjoyed family activities. In fact, her whole family had always enjoyed cooking together, and she quite comfortably spent a lot of time in the kitchen concocting new dishes in their company. Her father in particular enjoyed cooking.

Another thing Dina had always enjoyed was starting her day with a cup of hot chocolate. But shortly after her mother's heart attack, Dina walked into the kitchen one morning, looked at the package of powdered cocoa, and thought to herself that it was time to cut it out. She needed to lose weight. It was, to Dina, a lightning bolt thought. It felt as if her time had come. Dina didn't quite understand what that was about, but she went for it. Was it that she'd heard her mother now "had to watch her diet"? Possibly. Dina's mother was recovering but looked weak, and Dina was feeling a dull fear that shadowed her every day. This was partly due to the way her father had started to look. Thinner and worried.

At first she made the decision to cut out carbs for no other reason than that there were several diets people kept talking about, and carbs were the enemy. She never weighed herself. The numbers didn't matter a lot. It was how she looked. She became totally excited the day a friend said to her, "You look so skinny!"

Noticing that Dina no longer seemed to enjoy cooking with them and taking note of her change in weight, Dina's mother and father became concerned and took her to a nutritionist. The nutritionist made a point that there are "good" and "bad" carbs. Dina interpreted what the nutritionist said as meaning carbs can indeed make you fat.

Dina had entered not only the world of "everything is going to be great" but also "I hear the warning signs everywhere that something could stand in my way." "Boy was I ready to fight off the enemy! I found myself laughing a lot and being kind of unable to sit still. Something so great was around the corner."

Dina is very excited that she seems to have found a way to feel that all is going to be well with the world. Through magical thinking she has fixed on growing thin as a way of retrieving happiness. Even, perhaps, keeping at bay the fear that her mother could die. The heart attack and the resulting emotional upheavals had probably taken a heavy toll on Dina, and once she discovered that she could control her weight, she had likely invested it with the power to make things feel right again. This family may not actively be in a state of chaos, but certainly Dina has been through a frightening time and would naturally be seeking to feel things settle down. "I just knew I was headed in the right direction," she said. "No one could stop me!"

Dina's parents are most certainly in a tough spot. On one hand they have a daughter who seems to be feeling great. She hasn't, it appears, let life's vicissitudes get her down. She feels good about herself. Still, something isn't quite right. One day Dina's mother may think, "I'm not a worrywart. Look at my daughter! She's doing great!" The next, she may have that niggling feeling that Dina is not quite doing as well as she seems—that she is at times preoccupied, on another planet, almost giddy even for no particular reason. For a parent in this position, it's very hard to be sure about what is going on. But still, Dina's parents might want to pay attention to the following:

- Consistent behavior isn't always the telltale sign. If several days out of the week it seems to Dina's mother that Dina's behavior around food or clothing is odd, then she can note that. It probably means *something*. Whether or not she has to do anything about it will become obvious.
- Their daughter has been through a very emotionally difficult time. They may understand that the roots of most eating dis-ordered behaviors are emotional problems. The chances are likely that most everything Dina is doing or thinking has been or is affected by fear of losses (her mother's heart attack) she has suffered. In short, Dina may be more terrified than she is letting on.
- Any kind of even mild manic behavior is important to notice. It's often a cover-up for a great deal of anxiety. If Dina's behavior seems out of whack with her ordinary "up" moods, her parents might assume that there is something unusual going on with the dieting, especially because Dina has never been thinner.
- Children respond to silent messages as well as verbal ones. Dina sees her father's concern for his wife and may be taking it on as her own.

Even in this stage of "maybe she is in trouble, maybe she isn't," and even in the face of exceptionally happy and charged-up behav-ior, it is possible—and important—to at least note that things are different as well as *how* they are different. Getting lulled into believ-ing your daughter has never been happier—especially when you question her and she snaps, "I'm fine! Leave me alone!"—is very easy. It's not necessary to pounce, either. But you will want to stay alert and become gently active.

In Response You Can
- Be open to difficult conversations on emotional subjects. Your children need to know that talking about feelings can be

a great relief. In the process they will likely learn an emotional vocabulary that will serve them well for life.

- Invite your child to talk about what's happened in the family. While puttering around the kitchen you might say, "I can't imagine how you've been handling all this. There must be times when you have a lot of difficult feelings. Maybe you're sad, scared, and possibly even resentful. Whatever you're feeling, you are entitled to it." If she doesn't seem open to answering, you might want to add "Look, anytime you feel like talking, please let me know. Even if I'm reading or seem busy. I do want to know what's going on for you." In this way you will be working toward minimizing a repression of painful feelings that could feed eating disordered behaviors.

- If your child has been through difficult times at home, you might want to suggest a therapist with the idea that she can talk about how confusing and difficult things have been at home. You don't ever need to bring up the eating, although she might. "You know, I'm thinking I'd like to take you to see someone you can talk to. I have a feeling even though you look great and things seem fine, there might be something bothering you. I feel as if you're not eating properly, and you do seem awfully preoccupied at times." You needn't select an eating disorder specialist, but you will want to choose someone who deals almost exclusively with adolescents.

- Consider a visit to the pediatrician (see chapter 8). But be sure to present this as a move to keep her healthy and safe, *not* to stop her from dieting. "You've lost quite a bit of weight, honey, and I can understand how great that must make you feel, but I just want to make sure you're giving your body what it needs to stay healthy. Maybe the doctor can give you some information that will help you with the diet and at the same time be sure your skin stays clear and your hair shiny. Diets can affect those things, you know." Appealing to her desire to be attractive is not a bad way to get your child to the doctor.

- Without comment or argument (or added work for you), try adding nutrition to her diet. If you notice that she frequently says at dinner, "I'm not hungry. I'll just eat the salad," try pulling out some fresh sliced turkey meat, which you can easily buy at the deli, and say, "Okay, but why not add this? It's nothing but protein." Keep your voice relaxed and your words free of any criticism or excessive worry.

- If you are having trouble handling your own difficult emotions, it's important to get help. This is not just for yourself but also for the sake of your children. They are divining rods for a parent's unspoken feelings, and while it is perfectly okay to allow your children to see that you are human, it becomes problematic if your particular emotional state is troubling and upsetting for them. In some instances it simply may not be enough to say, "I'm upset right now, but I'll get over it." Recognizing your own need for help can only serve everyone's interests.

The following scenario is different from the others so far presented, as it introduces eating disordered behaviors into an actively chaotic and alcoholic family. Much work needs to be done to help this family, but the suggestions after this story represent how one might deal with the exhilarated dieter who is clearly suffering with a very difficult situation, besides her dieting, that is beginning to consume her as well.

THE NOT QUITE GOOD ENOUGH EXHILARATION

Ali had never felt as if she fit in. In fact, she couldn't really remember a time when she'd felt good. Depression seemed to dog her constantly. She had a circle of friends, but they weren't the popular crowd. Not even close. She didn't confide in them. Ali didn't think they'd "get it." Ali stayed home almost every weekend. Her parents were European, and nothing about them seemed like the other parents. They both worked in midlevel positions in banking, and her father was what is sometimes referred to as a "functional alcoholic" (that is, he is an alcoholic but can still handle some responsibilities). He was given to rages when he drank too much. Her parents also fought a lot, and Ali was an only child. Ali didn't like inviting her friends over to the house for fear of the scene they might witness.

Ali was around 15 years old when a girl, not someone she was particularly close to, commented on her thighs. "Isn't it funny," the girl said pointing to her own skinny thighs, "how each of us is built differently?" At first, Ali was stunned. She hadn't really worried about her thighs before. She thought they were fine. She had bigger problems.

But almost immediately "as if a bell went off," Ali decided to diet and get, as she put it, "very healthy." Her first move was to knock out all fast foods. Her second was to exercise. There was a big football stadium at her school, and she slowly worked her way to running up and down the stairs twenty times every afternoon. It took a few weeks. In addition to fast foods, she also began to eliminate anything with fat from her diet. For a week at a time she would call herself a vegetarian. But she was still eating.

Ali began to feel better. Excited. But not elated. She still couldn't seem to find her way into the popular crowd. Sometimes, in fact, she ate lunch all by herself, which began to be a good thing, as she didn't have to do any explaining about why celery and a slice or two of turkey was sufficient. Actually, her problems and her diet seemed to mesh nicely. That thought made her smile. Becoming gloriously thin was aided by her lack of close buddies.

Meanwhile, Ali's excellent grades continued. Noticing how much she was slimming down, her father started to compliment her. He praised her for her discipline. He acknowledged how thin she was getting, making it clear that he thought it an excellent move. Her mother, on the other hand, was worried, constantly asking if her daughter felt well. Ali consistently replied that she felt great, and her mother would nod and walk away only to return a few days later with the same question.

Soon Ali decided to eliminate carbs. That decision for a while heightened her sense of success. Still, though, she didn't feel quite right. And so on weekends after following a very strict diet all week, Ali began to *drink—on Saturdays only. Just a little. Her father had quite a stash. She told herself it was all right. She knew about the calories, but it couldn't be the same as food, she reasoned. After all, one drinks it.*

By this time, at 5'3", she'd dropped from around 114 to 99 pounds. She liked that number. It didn't have three digits. She considered stopping there but wasn't sure how to do that without going back up to 100.

Ali is a good example of a depressed adolescent who does not feel as if she fits in anywhere. She comes from an emotionally unavailable family with many relational problems complicated by cultural issues. Her parents do not get along, and her father is completely unpredictable with violent fits of rage. (He never hit anyone. He confines himself to hurling insults and objects.) He admits to drinking too much "on occasion" but denies being an alcoholic. Ali feels completely lost in her family and very out of place outside of it. Ali has no place and no one to lean on. But she has a good deal of personal strength and wants to succeed in both academics and sports. Due to cultural differences, her parents may not have seen the signs of Ali's distress, but they might have considered this:

- The fact that they did not grow up in the United States may leave them at a disadvantage in terms of recognizing troubling behavior. They may not recognize a normal diet for an American teenager, or they may be blind to the world of seemingly exciting diet options available to her. However, if they sense instinctually that their daughter is troubled, it is important that they educate themselves.
- It is rather unusual for a teenager to stay home most weekends. This is a time for children to begin developing meaningful relationships outside of the house. A teen who has no friends is likely a teen who is experiencing isolation and depression.
- When there is an alcoholic in the family, life at home can be unpredictable and chaotic. This is a situation that can wreak

havoc with an adolescent's sense of well-being and security. The need to control something can increase.

- The tendency for alcoholism may be hereditary. A depressed teen may easily decide to self-medicate. There is a lot of cover-up in an alcoholic family, and a child who is swept up into the deceit, the hiding, and the secrecy is a child who may stay isolated and introverted and devise all kinds of ways to comfort herself. In Ali's case, it is eating disordered behaviors and a flirtation with alcoholism.
- When adolescents claim to be vegetarians, it's worth watching what exactly it is she eats. This claim is often an excuse to not eat a variety of foods because of a diet.
- If a child asserts that "I won't eat anything that has a face," then watch to see if she will eat rice, pasta, potatoes, etc. If she refuses a former favorite food, there is likely a problem.

We included Ali's story for two reasons. First, her parents are not familiar with teen culture in America or even the world of help available in the area of mental health. Thus, they may not have understood the degree of her problem or, if they had, may not have known what to do about it. They are likely out of touch with other parents and so have nothing to which to compare their daughter's behavior.

Second, alcoholism is prevalent in our society and is a dangerous addiction. Alcoholism often promotes an atmosphere of secrecy and passivity within the family. This not only models the wrong approach to handling a problem with food but also saps the emotional and psychological energy of family members. Often children living in alcoholic families feel different than and cut off from their peers who appear not to be living with such a painful secret. A desperate desire to "fit in" or a need to feel in control of an out-of-control situation (addictions by their very nature render control elusive) can lead to excessive dieting.

In Response You Can

- If you are a family unfamiliar with the American teen, it is important to educate yourself. This can be done by talking to school guidance counselors or pediatricians or by introducing yourselves to other parents. Attending school meetings about various issues—from an information session on standardized tests to planning an event around the holidays—will help a great deal.

- If alcoholism is present in your family, it is critical to talk openly about the drinking problem with your daughter. There are many books out there on this subject.

- Help your daughter make the connection between the pain at home and her emerging chaotic eating patterns. "Honey, I know Dad's drinking is a real problem. I think it must be extremely upsetting to you, and I'm wondering if the way you are eating right now is an expression of how bad you feel inside. Sometimes when people get very anxious or unhappy, they try to find something to concentrate on to make things better. I'm wondering if that's what you are doing."

- Educate your daughter as to the genetics of alcoholism. Say it straight out. "You might have inherited a gene that leaves you vulnerable to becoming an alcoholic. This means that you have to be extremely careful about drinking. Frankly, I think you shouldn't ever touch the stuff, as it could be more dangerous to you than to other people." You might also add that it is in many ways a method of self-medication to take away bad feelings. Connecting alcoholism and excessive dieting in terms of their capacity to seemingly bring relief could drive the point home. Wonder aloud if her incessant dieting isn't somehow calming her as well. Let her know that if she does feel terrible sometimes, it might be a good idea for her to see a therapist who is trained to help people handle their problems in a way that can make life feel better.

- If your daughter balks when you express concern for her diet-ing—stating something like "This is the first time I've ever felt decent. I don't think you ever want me to feel good!" (a very common statement for a depressed adolescent)—specif-ically assure her that you are entirely concerned about her emotions. "Actually, your feelings are the things I'm most interested in. I'm wondering if you have angry or sad feelings, or any others for that matter, that are getting in the way of you seeing that you don't need to lose any more weight. I know you want to look good, and you do. But I'm worried about your emotional and physical health." When dealing with a teen, note the importance of *not* sounding as if you know exactly what she is feeling. First of all, you don't. And second, she'll resent the assumption. They're her feelings to be revealed when she is ready.

- If you notice that your daughter seems to be "hiding out," see if you can interest her in either a club at school or an outside class. Sometimes adolescents at school can become invisible to others, as they have not put themselves "out there." It's a role they get stuck with and often can't easily break away from. By introducing her to a new group of kids her age, she may be able to gain the social confidence she needs and bring a stronger sense of herself back to school.

- A word about triggers. You cannot control them. A depressed or anxious teen who is susceptible to the remarks and criti-cisms of others and who is dying to fit in can easily start down an eating disordered path if even one upsetting remark is made. But what you can do is acknowledge the intensity of her dieting and talk generally about how difficult it can be to deal with the pressure from outside. "You know, I can see how earnest you are about this dieting. I've never seen you like this before, and I was just wondering if anything is going on at school or among your friends to get you so charged up. It's really easy sometimes to be influenced by things people say or do, even if we don't like what's going on. Everyone wants to fit in and be admired." If she says that nothing is up and actually the dieting feels great, you might want to add, "You know, if anyone ever says anything to you that feels bad, I hope you'll discuss it with me. I won't laugh, and I won't get angry. I want to help you make sense of it. That's all."

Clearly the exhilarated dieter is extremely pleased with herself, though not totally consumed by her newfound sense of control. At worst she is at least highly motivated to keep dieting, as she is quite aware that to do so relieves the intensity of other problems. There is, in other words, some continuum of awareness still at this stage that dieting isn't everything and that, to greater or lesser degrees, it's making other problems more bearable. She does not necessarily feel the need to go any further, but the problem is that she may not know how to stop, both practically speaking and emotionally. The fear of "gaining it all back" could be overpowering.

The exhilarated dieter is at the surface a very self-satisfied if not happy dieter. It is important not to be seduced by her apparent good mood. This isn't easy. Adolescents can be moody, and when they're not they can be great fun; it's natural not to want to rock the boat. So don't rock it immediately. Just watch it, occasionally reaching out to keep it steady. And don't forget to admire *everything* about her. Now is an important time to consistently drive home the idea that thinness is not an important personal quality.

seven

Stage Three

The Obsessed and Preoccupied Dieter

As noted earlier, the shift from stage one, the innocent dieter, to stage two, the exhilarated dieter, is a subtle and seemingly positive one. Moving from the innocent to the exhilarated stage can be likened, for the adolescent, to a success story. It *is* exhilarating, and thus the emotional backdrop tends to be largely one of happiness and triumph, even if the eating behavior is getting more problematic. However, those adolescents in stage two who start moving into an increasingly more intense dieting pattern can become worrisome. Although this dieter is enjoying herself (albeit at times with some emotional and physical discomfort), her parents may be in a perpetual state of confusion, pleased for her happiness yet worried about her health and changing appearance.

In stark contrast, the emergence of stage three is readily apparent. The obsessed and preoccupied dieter presents, to the objective eye, a more clear-cut picture. For the teen, it can mark the turn into what might best be described as persistent emotional and physical mild distress, with potentially more serious problems to come.

Before, the diet seemed to enhance her life. Now, it's ruling the roost and creating a host of annoying, disturbing, unpleasant, and dangerous dilemmas.

Now hunger is an ever-present issue with which to reckon, and the logistics of dieting are beginning to infringe on the ebb and flow of life both with friends and at home.

For the previous two stages, we laid out "In Response You Can" lists in order to help you tease out the clues. With an obsessed dieter, we're no longer talking about clues; symptomatic behaviors are now on full display. Therefore, it is more expedient for us to list below what you are likely to see, simply as a kind of reinforcement for what you will likely already know. There is a significant problem afoot.

Your adolescent may

- Not want to go to certain restaurants for fear of there not being anything on the menu she can eat.
- Avoid social gatherings with friends if it includes soda, snacks, pizza, etc.
- Consistently play with the food on her plate, cutting things into tiny pieces, rearranging the food, and sometimes even attempting to dispose of some of it without anyone knowing it.
- Create tremendous tension at the dinner table due to her refusal to complete her meal and her lack of communication.
- Feel driven to go the gym, forsaking other interests.
- Begin to lose traction at school. Her grades and general concentration may begin to slip due to the effects of nutritional deprivation and eating-related preoccupation.
- Be more irritable and moody and experience depression, as indicated by an inability to attain a peaceful sleep and a tendency toward tearfulness.
- Often stare into space in a vacant fashion.

The obsessed and preoccupied dieter will usually, at the beginning of this stage, have some sense of how overwhelmed she is by the rules she is increasingly imposing on herself. She may actually realize that she's getting too thin but can't find the strength to combat what has become an obsessive and chaotic pattern of eating.

The preoccupation may not be with her all of the time, but it does pop up at various points during the day, and even she may find them exhausting. If her dieting continues unchecked, however, this modicum of self-awareness may begin to melt away, bringing her dangerously close to the brink of a diagnosed eating disorder. The risk of such an outcome is heightened if she begins to actively experience clear distortions in her thinking, insists that she's not thin enough, and worries incessantly about the risk of putting on weight. She may think that she is not trying hard enough and actually begin to view food as an enemy—an enemy that tortures her through obsessive thought. Yet in an apparent irony, at least from the perspective of others, she may be absorbed by menu planning, cooking for others, reading cookbooks, or collecting menus. As time goes on, this dieter may become increasingly desperate to thwart hunger, setting in motion a vicious cycle of increased hunger, restraint, and obsession.

When the obsessed and preoccupied dieter reaches a weight medically considered significantly below normal for her age and height, she may be diagnosed with anorexia nervosa. The following details the point at which a person fully meets all diagnostic criteria for anorexia nervosa:

- Weight drops to less than 85 percent of what is recommended for age and height, and there is a refusal or inability to maintain weight at or above this minimum.
- Weight takes on undue significance in regard to self-concept (meaning that self-satisfaction appears to hinge exclusively on weight loss or extreme thinness).
- She sees herself as large, in complete contradiction to her emaciated appearance.
- There is an apparent indifference to the consequences of the extreme weight loss.

It is important to remember, however, that just because your daughter seems to have entered this third stage does not mean she will decline into anorexia nervosa. Many adolescents who have trouble with eating come to the brink and realize, usually with some professional help, that it's time to stop the extreme dieting. Still, she may allow herself to become physically and psychologically compromised.

The physical effects of food deprivation are many, including fatigue, poor concentration and attention, insomnia, lowered body temperature and feelings of coldness, slowed pulse, reduced blood pressure, unease, depressed mood, and irritability. Now whole meals must be skipped, because eating with others is an anxiety to be avoided; she has lost her ability to moderate her behaviors and emotions.

Bingeing and some purging can emerge in stage three (though there may also have been some in stage two). While many adolescents try purging early on, it tends to be highly sporadic—a "technique" to turn to if they cannot help themselves after a particularly big meal or junk food splurge.

Now, however, the situation is different. She is extremely hungry. Her body is craving nutrition, so she may need to give in to her body's demands more often.

BINGE EATING AND PURGING

It's important to remember that we are not covering bulimia nervosa in this book, because as soon as bingeing and purging become a regular pattern, the adolescent is not on the brink. She has started to show frank signs of an eating disorder.

Occasional bingeing and purging, however, does sometimes appear as a subtype of anorexia nervosa. Likewise, in stages two and three of the slippery slope, bingeing and purging behaviors can appear. But this is most likely to appear in the third stage when the adolescent is likely exhausted from hunger and growing more desperate to attain or maintain a certain weight no matter how unreasonable.

The acts of bingeing and purging are separate acts, each of which can immediately produce shame and guilt. Both are usually done in secret and are experienced as immediate safeguards against putting on weight. They are, for most adolescents, embarrassing solutions. Purging can feel like a necessary evil (and not one to advertise), while bingeing can often leave adolescents disgusted with themselves, as they might feel that it shows a pathetic lack of control. This is why, as you will see, it is critical to remain calm and keep any conversation as empathic as possible. An aghast "What are you doing?!" will only further humiliate an adolescent who is already emotionally distraught.

Binge eating has two elements. One is a loss of control, which means that once eating commences, the person cannot effectively stop. Because of the loss of control, the amount of food that is consumed by the time eating terminates is excessive—more than what a healthy teen eats in a meal of normal size. Then, to counteract the effects of the food ingested, vomiting is self-induced or large amounts of laxatives are consumed under the mistaken belief that laxatives will actually prevent calories from being absorbed and thus reduce the likelihood of weight gain. Extended fasting may follow to "cancel out" the calories.

Binge eating is often, but not always, proceeded by a period of prolonged dietary restriction. Frequently, it arises when, in the midst of dieting, the person experiences life stresses that makes it difficult to sustain dieting behavior. The result is a rebound of overeating to compensate for restriction and to self-medicate an emotionally troubled state.

Binge eating and purging are typically done in secret, which makes detection difficult. The warning signs parents can take note of include:

1. Food inexplicably disappears.
2. The pace of eating is unusually rapid.

3. The meal doesn't seem to have its usual endpoint; that is, the teen seems to linger at the table, picking at food, or appears unusually preoccupied with eating something else.
4. Remnants of food eaten are found in the bedroom, sometimes hidden out of sight.

Binge eating can have its start in very subtle ways with a child who eats whenever she is upset. She is using food to soothe herself, to avoid feelings that are difficult to tolerate. This method of self-medication can eventually become normalized in a child's life. Thus, if and when she decides to diet, and does so successfully at first but is then unable to make it stick, bingeing can become a two-part solution. She can satisfy her hunger, and emotionally, through overeating, camouflage her negative feelings about herself. Concerned about the risk of weight gain, however, purging or heavy laxative use may emerge to compensate for the binge. With the cycle established, guilt and shame will follow.

Lizzie had a problem. She'd never liked her thighs. Starting in sixth grade, she began trying all kinds of diets in an effort to lose fifteen pounds, but she couldn't stick with them. She considered it to be her only personal weakness. She knew herself to be smart and outgoing. Lizzie had lots of friends (all of whom she consistently noted were thinner than her), and all of them upon entering eighth grade were now interested in boys. By ninth grade Lizzie had become obsessive about counting calories, looking up crash diets online and using the treadmill. She would lose around five pounds and then slip off the diet and slowly gain the weight back. She also took to reading food journals, though she was unclear why. As she put it, "I didn't want to think about food at all, but on the other hand it was one of the only things I was really interested in." But in tenth grade Lizzie began seriously slimming down, and at 5'8" her weight fell to 110 pounds. She recognized that she was now very thin but was petrified of putting back even one pound.

Lizzie was often extremely hungry, however, so she would occasionally binge. By her own estimations she could eat around fifteen thousand calories in one sitting. She was horrified whenever this happened, so she began to purge in the hope that this would keep her from gaining weight. About once every two or three weeks, Lizzie would be unable to manage her hunger pangs and would thus resort to bingeing and purging. Lizzie's parents traveled a great deal for work and often were not home at the same time. Hers was an emotionally inhibited family, and Lizzie hadn't learned how to speak up. This made it difficult for her parents to spot a troubling pattern. When her mother first saw the binge behavior, she heaved a sigh of relief thinking, "Thank goodness. She's not dieting anymore." But after it happened a few times, she began to realize that the periodic consumption of large amounts of food was actually a signal that something even more troubling than obsessive calorie counting was happening.

One evening after her parents ordered in a veritable feast of Chinese food, they watched as Lizzie gobbled down enough sesame chicken to feed an army. Lizzie then excused herself practically before the dishes were off the table, and it occurred to her mother to follow Lizzie to make sure she was okay. She heard the familiar click of the bathroom door and then moments later the unmistakable sound of purging, and she suddenly realized this was not the first time Lizzie raced to the bathroom after she ate a big meal.

Efforts to attain our culture's ideal can result in sustained attempts at food deprivation with the goal of extreme weight control. Adolescents who are constantly surrounded by rich, fast, and extremely appealing foods can, if they are dieting, feel hopelessly and helplessly deprived. It is easy to fall off a diet in this environment, an action that can lead to a sense of defeat or failure. Bingeing and purging can, under these circumstances, easily take on the mantle of a solution. While these behaviors are more likely to appear in stage three, there can even be experimentation with purging as early as stage one. There is, unfortunately, a kind of vogue surrounding the act. Teens will on occasion "wear it" like a badge.

It is essential that you understand how exhausting and shameful an episode of bulimic-like behavior can be for your child. The bingeing has, to say the least, made her both physically and emotionally uncomfortable. It is likely a consequence of prolonged efforts at restricting her diet, resulting in craving, and troubles at the emotional level that can both disrupt dietary restraint and create the need for self-soothing. However, it is also true that most sufferers are relieved when there is no longer a need to be secretive. There are several things that you should keep in mind if you discover that your child is on occasion bingeing and/or purging.

In Response You Can

- Recognize how difficult the loss of control must be. "It must be very painful to have to eat the way you just did and then feel the need to throw it up. I can't imagine how upset you must feel."
- Recognize that the child may not simply be able to stop just because she's been discovered. "Obviously I want to try to help you, but I realize this isn't going to be easy for you. Still, I need to do my best to take care of you. I'm not expecting miracles."
- Be available to sit with your child after mealtime and before bed, to help serve as a shield against the desire to binge. And do tell her what you are doing. The secret is out. There is no room for any more secrecy. "If I kept you company after dinner and until you climb into bed, do you think it would help you fight the urge to binge?"
- Prime bingeing times are after school and before dinner. If your schedule allows, suggest that you be there when she gets home. If this isn't possible, see what you can do about getting your daughter company. Your adolescent will likely not want to consume so much food in front of a friend.
- Perhaps most importantly, you will need to collaborate with a therapist. If your child is committed to extreme dieting and is bingeing or bingeing and purging, it is an indication that dieting and the body ideal have become the central focus of

your child's life. This is not something you can or should handle on your own.

What follows is a look at three dieters who have moved into the obsessive dieting stage. They are all clearly exhibiting serious eating disordered behaviors. The question is, what will they do next, and will they step over the line into the territory of a full-blown eating disorder?

Suzanne, age 17, was a girl who got things done. She had always been proud of that. She was efficient, smart, and motivated. Suzanne was the oldest of three children and very much looked up to by her siblings. At 5'4" and 140 pounds, she was unhappy with her weight. Suzanne was socially active and had many good friends. She was involved in the yearbook, loved to sing in chorus, and was totally into the debate team.

Midway through her junior year in high school, she decided to get thin. She set a goal. Thirty pounds had to go. Then in classic Suzanne fashion, she set about the job of dieting.

She was great at it. She brought all the determination she carried with her everywhere to the task. She was hard working, disciplined, and conscientious.

And so the thirty pounds melted away. Something, however, went awry. The problem was that Suzanne couldn't let it go. She easily admitted that the dieting had become an obsession and readily conceded that it was irrational. It was, in fact, driving her "crazy." She was also quite insightful about how this matched up with the rest of her personality. As her mother said, "Sue does everything 110½ percent." Suzanne nodded vigorously at this description. Then she quietly added, "You do, too." Her mother was at first taken aback, then commented slowly, "It's true. But I think I know when to stop."

This was likely true. Suzanne was growing up in a family with very high expectations. But interviews revealed they also were a family who could kick back and relax. Not everyone had to be "on" all the time. Suzanne, however, didn't seem to believe this. It was, she thought, her job to be the best. She was on a roll. And so Suzanne couldn't stop dieting. Three months later her weight had decreased to 90 pounds. Unlike girls with anorexia nervosa, she saw herself as decidedly too thin ("I look disgusting"), did not fear weight gain, no longer took pride in her weight loss, and denied that it gave her any sense of discipline or accomplishment—a fact that most professionals involved in her case did not quite believe. She was referred to a dietician and given the very firm admonition that if she was not able to begin restoring her weight, slowly but steadily over the next two months, it would be necessary to consider hospital-based treatment to prevent more serious consequences of her behavior.

Suzanne has entered stage three. Despite the fact that she is unhappy with her own appearance, she seems unable to lasso her own unhealthy eating patterns. She has become obsessed with losing weight. Her intellectual self seemed to clearly recognize that she had gone too far. Her emotional self did not. There was, it seemed, a deep and abiding satisfaction and sense of safety in the continuation of a steady weight loss. Perhaps it reassured her of her ability to be successful in an ongoing way. In other words, while an A+ on an English paper gave her pleasure, the paper was over and she would immediately begin worrying about the next.

The diet could be an unending indication of her supremacy over a perceived weakness. Each day was yet another sign that she was on top of her nemesis—the constant threat of not being "disciplined enough."

In Suzanne's case, within three months of being warned, she restored her weight to 108 pounds and described less preoccupation and rigid dieting. She could offer no clear explanation of how her behavior became so deviant and had no feelings of being too heavy or out of control now that her eating was less rigid.

This turnaround is not unexpected for most adolescents with disordered eating behaviors. Once reality is spelled out and a firm boundary is set, most teens have the capacity to turn away from such excessively driven behaviors. It is as if having grabbed all of the "control," they suddenly realize they would feel better giving back just a piece of it—and in doing so the obsession with dieting lessens. Perhaps some adolescents are actually relieved once a parent says, "This isn't good. I'm stepping into this."

Katrina, a 13-year-old, had a long history of extreme, near-paralyzing shyness and a fear of social situations. She could not attend parties unless she was sure a friend would stand by her side. She even had trouble walking into school late for fear of the class turning and looking at her. As is true of many extremely shy people, she had an intense fear of being judged.

This fear placed her at serious risk when she began to notice how the other girls her age were talking about their weight. One girl commented on her arms, another her hips, and still another her thighs and behind. Each girl seemed to have her own very distinctive complaints, and so, after staring in the mirror for a lengthy period of time, Katrina decided that she too probably needed to drop some weight from her stomach. "I figured the other girls saw that my stomach stuck out a little. I mean, everyone has something!"

She announced to her concerned parents that she planned to drop a few pounds from her 110-pound, 5'5" frame. "That's not necessary," they told her. "You're plenty thin already." Her mother in particular was very worried because as a young girl she herself had dieted dangerously and in fact still struggled to maintain a healthy weight. She never discussed this with her daughter. But Katrina merely smiled at them tolerantly. She was very aware that her mother skipped meals, though they never spoke of it. She also thought they simply didn't understand her world. Besides, it was just a few pounds.

But as her weight dropped below 100 pounds, Katrina continued to hear the girls talking and somehow imagined herself as someone who, like them, still needed to work on her weight. She began to think more about the goal of losing than the actual amount of weight loss and became preoccupied with the need to be disciplined. Katrina was not happy. She felt consumed. Before she'd been overwhelmed by her fears of speaking out, of expressing herself. But now she felt overrun by the never-ending question, "Should I eat this?"

Katrina is operating within a great deal of "thin" machinery. First, there is the group of girls to whom she is much attached. They are all dieting, and whether or not they are heavier than her bears little importance. Katrina is a girl who against the backdrop of her extreme shyness is desperate to "fit in," to "be accepted," to "belong." She is also the daughter of a woman who exhibited as an adolescent—and who still struggles—with eating disordered behaviors. Indeed, Katrina's mother does not like to eat lunch, convinced that it would simply put on the pounds. Instead, she drinks a diet coke. Aware of the prevalence of eating disorders, she did conscientiously try to hide her own feelings about food from her daughter, frequently commenting whenever her daughter was home something like, "Oh, I had lunch earlier. It was delicious!"

It never occurred to her that Katrina knew the truth and that her daughter thought it normal to fib about food. She didn't realize that Katrina saw it like this: Didn't *everyone* worry about their weight? Wasn't that *secret* common?

Katrina was briefly hospitalized when her weight hit 90 pounds. She was not diagnosed with anorexia nervosa, but she was placed in the hospital because her symptoms were persistent and significantly impaired her functioning in general. With the help of the strict but supportive environment that included planned menus, careful monitoring of her food intake, and direct attention to her emotional pain, she quickly resumed eating appropriately balanced foods without any major fear of gaining back too much weight. Her preoccupations lessened, and she was able to maintain more normal eating. She did attend a shyness workshop that enabled her to develop some tools for coping with her social anxieties. She remains shy but more able to manage the trait and was able to befriend two other girls for whom weight does not take center stage in their lives.

In Katrina's case, genetics and social pressures were simply, for a finite period of time, too overpowering. The dieting became her security blanket. It was an easy and obvious way to identify with others and did not require her to develop the necessary social skills to cope with her shyness. She could communicate with her body canvas. The hospitalization, however, not only brought her back to reality but required that she begin to work on her true weaknesses. Once she had acquired other means of reducing her social anxieties, Katrina was able to adopt healthier eating attitudes.

Up until ninth grade Joanna had been a star soccer and volleyball player, a solid student, and a socially active young teenager. She was a pretty girl with long, dark hair and a warm, vivacious smile. However, unlike her mother who had been a ballet dancer, she was not fine-boned or super slim. She had, as one would have expected from her activity profile, a healthy athletic body.

Toward the end of ninth grade Joanna was invited to the prom by an eleventh-grade boy. With two months to spare, she suddenly decided to go on a diet, commenting, "You can't believe what the girls look like who are taking the limousine with us." Her parents expected that she'd drop around five pounds and be happy.

In fact Joanna had no particular goal in mind, but when she'd lost the five pounds she professed not to see a difference. She continued dieting because, as she put it, she was "determined not to feel less pretty than the girls in the limo."

Mealtimes quickly became a painful experience. Joanna wasn't sure why. She was, in her opinion, looking great. Almost just right. She picked at her vegetables and ate a few forkfuls of whatever protein was on her plate. Her father immediately grew short-tempered, which was, it turned out, how he usually behaved when upset. Joanna had been very close to her 17-year-old brother, but as the tension grew at the dinner table he began to withdraw, one day muttering under his breath, "You're crazy." In an effort to keep her parents from harassing her at the dinner table, Joanna would purposefully eat something before dinner (allowing her parents to see the food in her hand but unable to estimate how much of it she'd already eaten) and then claim she just wasn't that hungry anymore. When her mother tried to talk to her, Joanna would cut her off, saying, "Look at you. You're so thin it's unbelievable."

Joanna's father became extremely watchful. Every day he wanted an accounting of what she'd eaten. It became a daily fight. Joanna only felt more and more desperate to cling to her diet. Finally her father took Joanna to a nutritionist, but Joanna hated her. She was convinced that everyone's only goal was to make her ugly. She lied to the nutritionist about her food consumption, and while she followed none of what the professional suggested as an appropriate diet, Joanna did continue, through careful counting of calories, fat grams, and carbohydrates, to eat at least two very small meals a day, which to her was plenty. Her parents committed to searching for a therapist Joanna would listen to, but no matter who they found she detested them all; she thought they were all stupid and didn't know what they were talking about. However, she did continue to lose weight and finally was taken to a psychiatrist. Her weight had at this point fallen from 118 to 97 pounds.

The psychiatrist began his session with Joanna by telling her that if she did not begin the process of eating in a more healthful way, she would likely have to be hospitalized. But then he also asked her a question that no one had bothered to ask in a very long time. What's her dream? What would she like to accomplish?

She wanted to be an actress, she informed him. He nodded and seemed very interested. She was thunderstruck by his interest—his sense that her life could be more than just about what she ate.

They talked about the demands of acting classes, auditioning, and more. They spoke for a full fifteen minutes about everything but her eating disorder, except to note that all of this was going to take energy and a commitment from her to living in a healthy body that could tolerate the stress of her goals.

Joanna felt a little piece of herself begin to relax. She wasn't ready to start eating the way everyone wanted, but her attention had now turned slightly to her dream.

The obsession with weight and dieting can grow more intense when an adolescent has to do battle with those she perceives would stop her. This makes it quite difficult to ever *push* her into eating in a reasonable fashion. She has to come to this place herself, with a combination of empathic support and boundary setting from those she loves. And she certainly needs to be reminded that who she is as a person is far more important than her diet—which has come dangerously close to filling up her whole world. Ironically, while it is she who has allowed the obsession with weight to infiltrate every part of her life, and though she would do battle with anyone who tried to rebalance her focus, there is a piece of her that desperately wants to be something more.

Joanna's psychiatrist understood that Joanna still needed to acquire a feeling of self-regard, self-importance and rational self-regulation of her behavior. He also made it clear to her, however, that she was sitting on a precipice from which she needed to step away. And then, in a quiet, unassertive, and nonfrightening way, he gave her a way to do so. He reminded her of the other piece of her inner life—her dream for herself—that was still alive and well and hidden behind her obsession with food. He also made it subtly clear that in order for Joanna to chase that dream, she had to take control of her entire self. She could, as a first step to her dream, perhaps take an acting class, but not before she began to take care of her health.

Before Joanna left the psychiatrist's office, they'd struck a deal. In two weeks, if she'd gotten her weight back up to 100 pounds with the help of her nutritionist, he would discuss with her parents the idea of a local acting class so that she could begin in an unpressured way to start learning the craft.

In stage three, the most important thing parents can do is allow themselves, despite their fears, to be as cognizant as possible about how precarious things have become. At this point professional consultation is mandatory. However, asserting yourself with utter authority is not. In fact, stridently insisting on anything at this point might stand in the way of your child hearing you and understanding that there is little chance of you looking away or allowing her to continue on the path she seems to have now set for herself.

In Response You Can

- Point out what it is specifically about the current diet that is not acceptable. In contrast, describe in a matter-of-fact tone a few typical, normal meals, including types of food and amount to be eaten. "The other night you ate a few pieces of steamed broccoli and half a chicken breast. I know you skipped breakfast that day. Of course, I don't know what you did for lunch, but I'm betting it wasn't much. Here is what I think is healthier."

- Describe what you've observed about your child's eating behavior. How is the food cut? What is the pace of her eating? Has her conversation at the dinner table trickled almost to a halt?

- Point out how her mood has changed. She's grown more sullen or irritable. Give her an example of when her behavior seemed unnecessarily negative and out of sync with what was going on. If she seems to have poor concentration or is given to hollow stares, make sure you note these observations. "You have always had such a wonderful, lively sense of humor. But I haven't seen it lately. You seem angry a lot of the time. Remember last Saturday morning when I asked you what you were doing for the day? You snapped my head off for no reason. You said something like 'Why do you have to know?' Honestly, what kind of an answer is that?"

- Note that her relationship with peers has seemed to shift. There is less contact; she seems to hide in her room a great deal of the time; and the usual get-togethers have appeared to grind to a halt. "You've always enjoyed your friends so much. Lately you're alone a lot. This can't be fun for you, and it isn't like you at all."

- If school grades have slipped, point this out along with any comments you might have received from teachers.

At this point you have a two-pronged goal: to state without any uncertainty what it is you see that is of concern, and to do so without disparaging her diet. You want her to listen to you. She won't be able to do that if she suspects you have no regard for her goals or what is meaningful to her.

Again, it is critical that you step in and point out how things have gone astray. But you need to do so in a calm, matter-of-fact way—nothing strident or accusatory.

DON'T SAY: I have noticed you are eating only a carrot and a few bites of meats every night for dinner. This is simply unacceptable.

DO SAY: I realize you want to be slim. But for dinner the other night you ate only a carrot and a few bites of chicken. This can't go on. Your body needs more fuel than that. You *can* keep a slender figure and eat healthfully, and we'll help you find a way to do so.

DON'T SAY: Ever since you've been on this diet, your grades have been slipping. I can't allow this to go on.

DO SAY: You've always been a wonderful student, but lately I've noticed that your grades have been slipping. It seems like it started since your diet has gotten extremely restrictive. I am very sure they are related, and we have to talk about what to do next.

DON'T SAY: You've been a totally disagreeable person ever since you've been on this extreme diet. You haven't been hanging out with your friends, and frankly you've been acting like a hermit. It's alarming. This diet thing has taken over your life.

DO SAY: I've noticed that as your dieting has gotten more involved, you're spending more and more time by yourself. You've also been moody, and you rarely smile anymore. This is not good. It's time for us to figure out how you can feel comfortable with the way you look and go back to enjoying the life you had before your dieting got so extreme. I recognize you want to be thin, but thin and unhappy don't have to go together. You used to laugh so much. We need to help get you back there.

Remind her of where she used to be. Express your respect for her desires and concerns. But let her know that what is going on now has to stop and that *together* you intend to help bring her back to a state that is both physically and emotionally healthy.

A Note about Hospitalization

We've mentioned hospitalization a few times in this chapter. At times, if the problems associated with stage three cannot be brought under reasonable control with outpatient therapy, care in an eating disorder treatment program within a hospital setting may be required. The main purpose of this intervention is to prevent the continuing downward spiral into an eating disorder.

The major elements of this treatment are:

- Individual therapy and group therapy to examine the personal psychological and emotional factors fueling extreme negative attitudes about weight.
- Family therapy to address broader problems in the home environment.
- Structured meals and nutritional counseling to normalize eating behavior and correct distortions relating to weight regulation.
- Groups designed to teach healthy coping behaviors in order to reduce general stress and improve social skills.

The time required to reasonably achieve these objectives will vary and can never be easily predicted. It is important that the stay be of sufficient time to establish a solid footing in each of these areas, as treatments that are too brief in duration will frequently be followed by very rapid returns to the hospital. The length of time needed to address eating disordered behavior within a hospital-based program will naturally depend on factors such as weight at the time of admission and overall severity of the teen's mental state. If the weight is not dangerously low, the stay may be as brief as two to three weeks, at which point many programs rely on intensive outpatient care in order to continue treatment at the level needed to address continuing behavioral and emotional concerns.

WHAT THE RETURN TO NORMAL EATING MIGHT LOOK LIKE

Starting out, expect ambivalence. This is a word you will need to embrace.

Your adolescent is quite likely going to experience a good deal of anxiety about returning to normal eating patterns. What if she starts to look fat? Or feel sick? What if she can't stop obsessing about her weight or can't stay off the scale? What if you expect her to just start eating when she can hardly think past the five bites of chicken she's grown used to?

What if she just can't do it?

The road to healthful eating is bound to be a rocky one, with a few steps forward and hopefully fewer backward. The first time the scale begins to go up, she may experience mild panic, a sense that she is once again losing control. Or this feeling may not descend immediately but rather a bit later, after she hears a well-intended remark about how much healthier she is looking, which she may immediately construe as a euphemism for "fat."

It is important to remember that emotional factors such as low self-esteem and shame are operating when body dissatisfaction is high. The keys to helping your adolescent manage these feelings are:

1. Expressions of interest and understanding. "Can you tell me what you are most afraid of about adding a few important foods to your diet? I want to be clear about the things that scare you."
2. Consistency of support. "Please let me know whenever you are feeling frightened of eating your meal. Talking about it might help."
3. Kindness wrapped around a firm and unwavering hand. "I know this is hard for you, but we really need to get you back to a healthy place with eating. I also don't want you to be miserable while we work this out. I'm sure we can come up with a plan."

Initiating steps to contain the dieting clearly involves a heartfelt understanding of the complexities embodied in the eating disorder. But normalization of the diet is a must and will almost certainly at this stage require a series of consultations with a qualified nutritionist who can structure a meal plan that is balanced in regard to nutrients and calories. The plan will take into account your adolescent's ambivalence and thus in a measured way slowly move her toward a healthy relationship with food. To this end, the nutritionist should work closely with you and your teen in order to create a plan that takes into account her emotional and physical needs as well as put into place a method of assessing your child's compliance.

Indecision, reluctance, stubborn refusal, obstinacy, fits of anger and protest, and panic are all potential roadblocks depending on how much disturbance in attitudes there is and the degree of risk for actual eating disorders.

You will need to anticipate in advance the potential for anxiety, help your child anticipate this as well, and discuss possible strategies for managing it. These may include:

- Sitting together after meals to talk.
- Generous reassurance during the meal.

- A quiet stroll after dinner.
- Learning and practicing relaxation techniques together.

Your consistent support and understanding will be crucial as your child struggles to return to a healthful eating pattern. She *can* do it. But try to remember that it was a complex group of variables that got her to this difficult place. The way out is bound to be equally intricate. The chapters that follow will help you not only choose the right professionals for your particular situation but also help you with some tools for helping your child, once she has achieved a semblance of normal eating patterns, to stay there free of rampant anxiety and fears.

Your child may be on the brink of an eating disorder, but as the title of this book suggests, there is much you can do to pull her back to a healthful place.

eight

Seeking the Help of Others

"*I sat in the living room with my head in my hands. My daughter Debra had just left for school, leaving behind a piece of toast from which she'd taken one bite. She had an apple in her hand that I knew she wasn't going to eat. The apple, essentially, was for me. It was part of her attempt to paint a picture of good nutrition that I might hang on the wall along with our family photos. I felt beaten down. I'd tried talking to her, yelling at her; I used understanding words and threats. I'd shopped differently, I'd cooked differently, and I'd even dieted with her in an attempt to model how it should be done. My daughter was growing more and more clever each day, twisting and turning her way past food—and me.*"

It isn't easy to recognize when outside help is necessary. As parents, we all want to believe that *we* are enough to help our children. We brought them into this world, and we should know how to keep them safe. From tightly holding their hands in busy shopping malls, taking them for regular doctor appointments, and speaking to teachers on their behalf, we've done our best to be there for them. We've comforted them over fights with friends or a broken heart, eased their fears as they faced new academic and social

159

challenges, and set curfews and rules to give them both independence and boundaries. We've tried to be everything our children need us to be.

It's important to remember here that none of us can meet all of their needs. There are powerful influences everywhere that can sometimes wash over us and our children like tidal waves, and when we come up for air it is apparent that we are simply not powerful enough, on our own, to put everything back to order. We need help. The most important thing in a situation like this is to *recognize* these moments, even if you don't act on things immediately. Indeed, you don't have to jump the moment it hits. You may need time to allow yourself to see the situation clearly. In fact, leaping too soon could be detrimental to your relationship with your child. But what you don't want to do is wait too long. Unfortunately, waiting too long often happens. It's not that parents don't see there's a problem, it's that we fear what it may mean and then hope against hope that it will go away on its own. We may think:

- I'm a bad parent.
- It will pass. She's just going through a stage.
- What if everyone finds out?
- If I can't help her, we must have a terrible relationship.
- If I wait long enough, she'll talk to me. I'm *so* open.
- This is a family matter.

All of these concerns are understandable yet unfair to everyone involved. We do not control the universe, and when there's a problem that we can't resolve or that isn't resolving itself, we have to admit to our limited capacity to help. The most important thing we can do is remain solid role models, good advisors, and ever-present supports. And then get help.

If your child is dieting in a problematic fashion, what matters most is to get you, your child, and if appropriate your family the help that is needed to bring your daughter back to a healthy place.

The good news is that there are professionals from a number of disciplines who can step in and help. This chapter will explore each of these specialties from several perspectives, but first here is a thumbnail sketch of who we're talking about.

Physicians. The role of the physician is to monitor a patient's general medical status, evaluating vital signs and general health status especially in cases when patients have been dieting restrictively or using vomiting, diet pills, laxatives, or diuretics to lose weight. A physician is also often the first person you might visit (given that yearly checkups are the norm and might coincide with you reaching out for help), and therefore he or she is the first objective judge as to whether your child is on an unhealthy course.

Dieticians and nutritionists. A dietician provides counsel and guidance regarding eating behaviors. When dieting becomes dysfunctional, it is often necessary for a patient to receive structured advice in meal choice and planning. A dietician or nutritionist will advise both you and your child.

Therapists. The therapist's role is possibly the most sensitive of the four we list here. It is this professional's job to identify and treat all aspects of the patient's and family's psychological difficulties and to provide treatment for dysfunctional eating attitudes and behavior. Choosing a therapist is a critical aspect of helping your child, who needs to be encouraged to participate in her therapy. In this chapter we will spend considerable time on this issue. We will also include a look at family and group therapies.

Psychiatrists. Psychiatrists may also serve in the role as therapist, but increasingly they serve as managers of a patient's medication in those cases where drugs are deemed necessary to treat clinically significant anxiety or depression.

WHO IS IN CHARGE?

At this point it is important that we address an extremely important question that you will need to keep in mind, especially if it becomes necessary to enlist the help of all of the above professionals. We cannot stress this enough.

You will need to establish who is in charge.

The management of a dieting crisis involves making general decisions about such matters as the ideal weight to maintain or to achieve when a teen is underweight and whether the teen should engage in extracurricular sports, participate in family vacations, etc. It is imperative that a single individual assumes responsibility for all general clinical decisions. You will want to immediately raise the question of who will direct the treatment. The ideal choice for this role—the coordinator of care—is a therapist. It is therefore important that the therapist you choose has specialized expertise in the care of people with abnormal eating behavior. This kind of training and experience will allow the therapist to provide guidance to other health professionals. You will want to know how the professionals are communicating and what the lines of communication are. Similarly, it is important to ask the professionals what they consider the boundaries of their individual roles to be (what will each be doing and what will be deferred to other members of the team). Although a psychiatrist is responsible for management of medication, it is important for the therapist to have a good general working knowledge of these treatments, what they indicate about a patient, and the potential side effects. The therapist also needs to be able to facilitate, if necessary, dialogue among the different professionals so that no important facts are lost.

Clearly there is a great deal of available help for an adolescent (and her or his family) with a potential eating disorder. There are also many things to keep in mind when pondering a visit to any one of the available professionals. Depending on the specialist, you might want to know how to choose, what you can expect, what questions to ask, how to prepare your adolescent, and, most certainly, warning signs that you are in the wrong place. Your instinct that your child needs your help is correct. Choosing the person(s) to contribute to your adolescent's emotional and physical health is a powerful way to fulfill your desire to keep your child safe.

THE PHYSICIAN

Most parents start here. We are familiar with our pediatrician and feel most comfortable presenting sensitive concerns in her or his office. Your child will likely feel most comfortable here as well. It would be wise to give the pediatrician a call in order to indicate your concerns before you arrive with your child. Clearly a bad approach would be to walk in and announce, "She's not eating. Look at how skinny she is." But surprisingly so is, "We're here because Bonnie and I see her eating habits differently. I don't think she's eating enough, but she thinks her diet is fine." Few adolescents would fail to read the subtext, which is, "Okay. Tell us. Who's right?" And many pediatricians who do not have a specialized working knowledge of eating disorders may miss the point entirely.

Rather, speak to the doctor in advance, and upon arriving at the office and before your child actually goes in for an exam, simply say right in front of your child something like "She's dieting and I want to make sure she's healthy." In this way, you won't be skirting the issue, you won't be asking the doctor to take sides, and you will be placing "health" on the table—not who is right or wrong.

How to Choose

Your child already has a pediatrician, so it is unlikely that you will want to go shopping around at this point for one who is particularly familiar with eating disordered behaviors. However, you should be aware that even the finest of pediatricians may not be particularly knowledgeable on the subject. This is important to keep in mind during that previsit phone conversation. There's no harm in asking the doctor if he or she has dealt with children who have eating disorders, whether he or she is familiar with the signs, and how he or she usually talks about them with patients. Doing so with concern in your voice may serve to inspire the pediatrician to think through what he or she knows, talk with colleagues, and at the very least take extra care in the way in which he or she deals with your child. A child who is slim but not too much so might prompt a harried doctor to say, "You're fine. Go eat a chocolate bar." This is not as likely to happen if you draw the pediatrician's attention to your concerns in advance.

What to Expect

Your child's doctor should do appropriate blood and urine work specific to the concerns of repercussions from poor eating habits, perhaps do a bone density test, check the height and weight trajectories, and cover other basic elements of a physical. He or she might also be prepared to explain how nutrition, in general terms, affects sexual development, height, athletic performance, appearance (hair and skin), and more. This would be wise, given the deep concern adolescents have about their appearance and prowess. Your child might even listen. If your instinct tells you that right now this doctor is the only professional your child will see, and things are not too out of hand with her weight (as established by the doctor), you might talk over a plan in which she can make appointments for regular weigh-ins.

If your child's weight continues to fall, it's fair to expect her physician to express concerns to her that issues beyond her weight may be at play and then strongly suggest that she make an appointment to talk to someone. But as with all things, this requires some pacing. No adolescent will tolerate feeling bulldozed.

Warning Signs
- Obviously, if your child has never liked her pediatrician and balks at the idea of going to the doctor for a checkup, now is the time to switch and find an adolescent specialist who is well informed about eating disorders. Any child who does not have a positive feeling about her doctor should not be scheduled for an appointment with him or her at this highly sensitive time. An appointment rife with mistrust would be far

more detrimental than losing the familiarity factor. Instead explain the switch this way: "I found you a doctor who only sees kids your age. I think it will be easier to communicate."

- Beware of the careless remark. Remember, many doctors are pressed for time. Put this together with a doctor who is not accustomed to focusing on potential eating disorders, and thoughtless comments or snap decisions could result.

> "When I was about 15 my mother took me to the doctor. I was really thin. I was really pleased. I was extremely anxious they'd force me to do something I didn't want to do. The doctor pinched my side and said, 'There's still enough meat on you!' My mother looked perplexed.
> I got worried about the meat."

Other common missteps might look like a doctor who

- Doesn't ask your child about her diet but rather breezily remarks, "Start eating a few desserts."
- Smiles and say, "You still have plenty of weight on you."
- Hands her a piece of paper upon which a healthy diet is printed and says, "Here, follow this"—as if the problem is that she doesn't know how to eat.

If you feel as if your doctor is missing the boat, you might wait a bit, hoping the visit itself will turn your child around; if things continue to worsen, then switch to someone new and explain that you just want to get a second opinion; or schedule a visit with a nutritionist. Here you might say, "Look, if you're going to diet, at least let's make sure you're going to stay healthy while doing it." Again, it's a statement that says, "I'm on your side."

THE DIETICIAN OR NUTRITIONIST

Nutritionists and dieticians are schooled, among other things, in the facts about calories, metabolism, and the body's nutritional needs. Ironically, your adolescent knows a great deal about these issues, too. The problem is that she only cares about staying thin or losing weight. And so, having made a study of the calorie, fat, and carb counts on all foods combined with the basic knowledge of how our bodies burn "fat," she has created a perfect diet to suit her psychological, *not* physical, needs. A little knowledge can be a dangerous thing. This is why handing your child a well-planned diet on a piece of paper is a waste of time. The prism through which she is viewing food is distorted, created to serve the purpose of weight loss at any price.

Eating disturbances are not due to a paucity of information about healthy diets. They have far more to do with an inadequate understanding of how the body works (and thus healthy ways to manage weight), psychological issues that keep adolescents from considering the facts, and the attendant chaotic eating patterns that are difficult to break. This is where nutritionists can help.

What to Expect

Different nutritionists have different styles of working, and much of their approach will depend on the particular client. A nutritionist may choose to see you and your daughter together at least for part of the first session. This is to get each of your perspectives on the problem and to get a sense of what kind of dynamics exist between the two of you on the subject of food. She is *not* passing judgment. She is observing. She wants to hear your fears and the way in which your daughter counters them. She will be looking at how combative the two of you might become or whether the two of you tend to be more "still" around each other. She may ask you some questions about family history, which is an important piece of the challenge your daughter might be facing.

The nutritionist may also elect to see your child alone from the get-go and speak to you for the most part on the phone.

Nutritionists who work with adolescents can be most successful if seen by your child as *her* advocate. Confidentiality is important. Otherwise lies will abound. The nutritionist will likely tell your daughter that anything she tells her will be held in strict confidence unless she believes her to be in real danger. Then you will be informed. This is not to say that you cannot put in a call on a somewhat regular basis to see in general terms if your daughter is basically "with the program." But don't be surprised if after asking a question the nutritionist says something like "I really need to respect Sara's privacy."

Still, substantively speaking, it's important that you know the general range of topics the nutritionist will cover at least in part during each session she has with your child. Most people have a general sense about a "nutritional vocabulary," but misconceptions abound. The following brief explanations of each subject will help you ensure that you have a working knowledge of the terms being used.

Calorie. A calorie is a measurement of the energy released when your body breaks down food. The more calories in a food, the more energy that food can give your body. Thus, if you eat *more* calories than you need, your body stores the extra calories as fat. When we speak of a normal caloric intake range, this refers to the number of calories needed to *maintain* an approximate weight.

Ideal body weight. This is the desired healthy weight range, give or take five pounds for a person of your age, gender, and body frame.

Target body weight. This number generally refers to 90 percent of the ideal body weight.

Setpoint. This is the weight that your body always tries to maintain no matter how many calories you add on or take away. It is the weight at which you are most healthy. When you dip below this weight, the chemical reactions in your body slow down; muscle tone, body temperature, and blood sugar dips; and your heart muscle works at 50 percent of it's ideal rate.

Metabolic rate. This is the rate at which your body burns calories. It fluctuates on a regular 24-hour cycle. The metabolic rate increases during and after exercising.

Body mass index (BMI). This is the measurement used to determine if the amount of fat on your body is appropriate to maintain physical health.

The food pyramid. This serves as a guideline for a healthy diet. It is not rigid law. Ideally, it allows some flexibility to enjoy foods that suit one's lifestyle and preferences. There are five major food groups in the pyramid from which one should consume a minimum serving: (1) milk, yogurt, and cheese; (2) meat, poultry, fish, dry beans, eggs, and nuts; (3) vegetables; (4) fruits; and (5) bread, cereal, rice, and pasta.

Food exchanges. If food items in a nutrition plan are not to one's liking, you can substitute a different food from that same group. For example, if you do not want to eat red meat, you can substitute with tuna or salmon. Of course, proportions of nutrients have to be considered, and the nutritionist can help even things out in this area.

What Might Be Expected of You

Don't be surprised if at the end of the conversation you have with your child and the nutritionist you are given some "marching orders." For those nutritionists who strongly believe that parents need to keep their distance from the dieting, these might be:

- "Please put away all scales in the house."
- "Do not argue with your daughter about what she is eating. You are not the food police."
- "Make sure that everything on the food plan is in the house."

However, you may find a nutritionist who favors a more active family participation. In this case, the nutritionist will likely outline a list of do's and don'ts for you to follow.

How to Prepare Your Adolescent

Many teens who are displaying eating disordered behavior will balk at the notion of seeing a nutritionist. They anticipate a doctor of sorts whose only goal is to *make* them put on weight. While ultimately it is true that the nutritionist is interested in helping your child return to a healthful weight, he or she is not after a quick fix (which ultimately will only lead to an equally fast weight loss). The nutritionist is interested in your child's entire experience around eating and understands that your child will only regain healthy eating patterns if her fears, anxieties, and goals are understood and incorporated into the plan they devise together. Nonetheless, you do need to give your child some realistic expectations so that she feels relatively comfortable during the first visit and doesn't think anyone is "pulling a fast one" on her. In fact, you might want to liken the nutritionist to a kind of coach.

> "I did not actually feel that the nutritionist was on my side or my daughter's side. I got the distinct impression she was on my daughter's health side. I found that feeling to be very comforting."

You might want to tell your child that the nutritionist

- Will ask you to talk about the kinds of food you are eating, how much, and when.
- Will likely ask questions about any drug or alcoholic use.
- Will want to know about your friends and what habits they might have when it comes to food, drugs, and alcohol. Also, how do they feel about their bodies?
- Will likely need for you to think about any patterns of eating you might have. For example, do you like to eat in front of the television? Do you like to eat certain foods in a particular order?
- Will want to understand how you feel about eating. Does it make you feel frightened? Does eating some foods tend to make you feel fat or messy?
- Probably give you useful information. (Avoid the word "teach".) The dietician will explain to you how your body uses food and how much it needs. He or she will talk to you about such things as calorie intake, metabolic rate, and set-points. It's all part of gaining a better understanding of how to take care of your body even on a diet.
- Will likely help you create a food plan that you can live with.
- Will want to begin a conversation about target weight.
- Will encourage you to ignore numbers. You may be asked to stand on the scale backwards to take some "numbers" pressure off of you. He or she might suggest that you stop counting calories and carbs and fat grams but will encourage talking about healthy and important food groups. Serving size might come up as well.

Your child needs for her nutritionist to understand the ambivalence she has about eating. She needs to feel that this nutritionist is not going to try to *make* her do something she simply can't right now. A good nutritionist will work with your child to build on her strengths and gently educate her about her body's needs; she will also help her readjust her concept of what her body should look like. The nutritionist may also be the person you call if you see something going on that worries you. Instead of plunging into an argument with your daughter, you might say, "Let's call Patti and find out what she thinks of this. I don't know what to make of it myself."

The best way to work with your daughter's nutritionist is to let her do her job, and part of that job is giving you a chance to maintain a positive relationship with your child.

Another way to help is to listen to the nutritionist's advice about whether or not your child may need to see a therapist. We've already discussed many of the underlying psychological issues that accompany eating disordered behaviors. Your nutritionist is not trained to handle this aspect of your child's problems, but the nutritionist may feel that he or she can work most effectively in concert with a therapist. Ideally, both the therapist and nutritionist will find moments in which to tell your daughter the limitations of the work they each can do. For instance, a nutritionist faced with a client's highly emotional admission of some feeling or action might gently tell your daughter, "I'm glad you told me. But you know, discussing those issues is not the kind of work I do best. Would you feel comfortable telling your therapist instead? If you'd like I can help you do that." It will be made clear to your adolescent that if she needs both, there will be communication between these two professionals in order to make sure she is getting the best care possible.

THE THERAPIST

Adolescents who are exhibiting eating disordered behaviors are subject to a good deal of criticism and what they perceive as harassment from you and others who care about them. Most often the criticism is born of love, but it can feel like a frontal attack. Think about what they hear:

"This is crazy! Eat already!"
"Are you nuts? No one can eat this little?"
"I feel sick watching you eat."
"This is abnormal. It has to stop."
"You're ruining dinnertime for everyone!"

A child's refusal to eat a normal diet is frightening to parents, and in an impulsive desire to knock some sense into their child, the above statements come out easily and often. They are desperate attempts to get a child to "wake up." But for the eating disordered adolescent, these are threatening, frightening, and anger-producing statements; they give your child a "reason" to plunge even further into their problem.

Enter the therapist. Unlike you, as the parent, a therapist is not burdened with the love and emotion you feel toward your child. Therefore, the therapist is not driven to remarks that are alarming, insulting, or, despite your best intention, riddled with the fear of your own inadequacies.

A therapist exists in this situation to objectively help your child understand what is actually behind this quest for thinness. Why is her body image so painful? And what is keeping her in this difficult spot? At some point after a child's dieting enters a more dramatic sphere, there can be a sense of having "hit the wall." The adolescent can't stop obsessing about food, and the parent feels completely helpless against her pursuit of the "perfect" weight—whatever that might be. A therapist can help break the impasse.

What to Expect

How a therapist chooses to help your child sidestep the wall can vary. The therapist may opt for individual sessions with your daughter in order to try, in an atmosphere of confidentiality and through a one-on-one relationship, to help her uncover some of the difficult feelings that are driving the eating disordered behavior. The therapist may do so by exploring past problems and difficult patterns in the family or by sticking to more current issues. He or she might concentrate on whatever distortions in thinking your daughter is evidencing or might stress finding immediate solutions to problematic eating behaviors by helping your daughter isolate and then deal with difficult immediate challenges. The therapist may in fact draw from all of these approaches.

The therapist may also suggest family therapy to help resolve the problems. After all, it is within the family context that your child has grown up and is now living, and there are bound to be issues of communication and perhaps unhappy or frustrating family entanglements that need to be unraveled. Remember, the root of your child's problem is multifactorial, but the family unit certainly may provide an atmosphere in which conflicts, misunderstandings, hurts, and anxieties can exist. Your daughter needs a lot of support during this time, and in order for that to happen it's important to make sure the environment in which she is living is as conflict-free as possible.

The therapist may also suggest group therapy. In this approach, the therapist gathers a number of adolescents who are flirting with eating disorders and tries to have a group discussion of the common issues. At first this can seem a bit embarrassing to participants, but after a while it becomes clear that there is much to be gained by the support and understanding of other kids who are in a similar place. The therapist's role in this context is to facilitate conversation that will lead each child to greater understanding of themselves and to give each participant a chance to be supportive and helpful to the others—an important part of building self-esteem.

How to Choose

The choice of therapist is a critical one. You need to feel comfortable with this person's training, treatment approach, and communication style. Although the therapist will need to promise your child confidentiality—unless he or she feels that your child is in serious danger—you will still want a therapist who will offer you advice and maybe even comfort. Ask if the therapist will take your calls and answer basic questions. If you are worried about something, how available will the therapist be to speak with you? Would he or she be willing to see your whole family on some occasions? Will the therapist meet with you alone (if your daughter gives permission)?

Then, of course, you have to take into consideration your child's feelings and personality. Does it matter to her if this person is a male or female? Would she like someone young, middle-aged, or older? Would she do better with a therapist who is very active in the session, helping her to feel comfortable and formulate her thoughts, or would she work best with someone who took on a more subtle role? Perhaps your child would do best with someone who carefully observes her but takes a more passive stance, allowing her to come forward (or not) as she pleases. This is a stylistic issue that you and your daughter would need to assess together and that may not be decided until your daughter is actually in a therapeutic session.

Finally, you do need to be prepared to look around. You and your daughter may visit a number of therapists until you find one who feels right. This may take two or three appointments with each therapist. During each initial appointment, you will likely sit in for at least half the session. Upon the first meeting most people will report that the "right fit" feels like this:

- You experience the therapist as listening to and truly understanding your words and those of your child.
- You experience compassion emanating from the therapist.
- Your daughter feels comfortable in the therapist's presence.
- The therapist sounds confident and competent and openly explains the way he or she works.
- The therapist asks insightful questions.
- The therapist speaks to your daughter in a way that sounds genuine and respectful.

- The therapist clearly knows a lot about eating disorders.
- Neither you nor your daughter walk out of the therapist's office feeling frightened, put off, or tense.

A competent therapist with whom you can feel comfortable can help your daughter toward solutions. A poor match will only add to her anxiety and perhaps even increase her reluctance to let go of her eating disordered behaviors. If after a few sessions your daughter tells you she does not feel comfortable, discuss it with the therapist. You may want to find someone else with whom your daughter can better relate. However, if this happens with more than two or three therapists, it would be important to consider the possibility that your adolescent does not at this time really want any help. She may feel too threatened. Rather than *stop* therapy, this reluctance to reveal herself to anyone should likely become the first topic to focus upon *in* therapy.

However, if indeed your child is reluctant to try therapy, you might want to go instead for a few sessions to address the anxieties you are experiencing and to gain some insight into how to better relate to your daughter. The less combative your interactions, the more likely your child will listen to you. Once there is more trust, she may indeed give therapy a try, as it will no longer feel like a potential weapon you are using to stand in her way.

The First Session

The first session is a critical information-gathering session that will help give the therapist a context for your child's life and the issues with which she is currently dealing. It will therefore likely include time for you and your child together. The therapist will be interested in all kinds of background information: ages of family members, any history of psychological or physical illnesses in family members, the names of medical doctors you've seen, and whether or not there has been any form of abuse within the family. If you are separated or divorced, she will want to know the tenor of the relationship you have with your your child's father and the level of tension the family is currently experiencing emotionally and even financially. Some questions may seem simple, others unnecessarily intrusive, and some will be asked twice—once with you and your child together, and once when your daughter is alone. Substance abuse is an example. The therapist will want to know how your child responds to a question about her use of illegal substances in your presence and when alone with the therapist. The most important thing that you can do as a parent and that you should encourage from your child is to be as honest as possible.

How to Prepare Your Adolescent

If your daughter would like to see a therapist but is somewhat nervous about it, make sure she understands that you understand why she might be nervous and that you are going to try to see to it that she is comfortable in therapy. Make it clear to her that you are not going to ask her to see a therapist she doesn't like and with whom she feels she can't talk. Let your child know that she has some control over this process. She not only deserves it but also needs it. Otherwise, therapy will be fruitless.

If your daughter is reluctant to enter therapy, you might want to tell her that you sense she is struggling with problems you cannot understand and that you are finding the way in which she is managing food a little frightening. Tell her that you would like the help of a therapist to assess what's going on. Then, as above, indicate that you see therapy as a very personal thing and that you want to find her a therapist with whom she can feel comfortable. You're not simply going to stick her with a therapist her doctor recommends. You might also want to add that seeing a therapist is not a lifelong commitment and that all of you can discuss with the therapist how long a trial period might be.

Whether she wants to start therapy or not, your daughter will likely be a little anxious about the process. What will it be like? What will she be talking about? What if she can't talk or isn't in the mood to talk? What if she doesn't want to answer any specific questions?

The best answer to all of these concerns is, "These are all things we or you alone can talk about when we meet with the therapist. This is supposed to be your time. The therapist is a person who is going to help you understand yourself better. But to do that, the therapist has to try to get an understanding of you first. Ask whatever you need to ask. That will help the therapist get a handle on who you are." Then make sure your daughter understands the following things about a therapist-client relationship:

- Unless the therapist thinks you are in imminent danger, whatever you tell him or her will be held as confidential.
- The therapist will ask you lots of questions because he or she wants to understand who you are and how you got to be that person.
- The therapist is not going to be judging you or your actions. He or she is there to help you figure out why you might be engaged in behaviors that aren't good for you and then find ways to help you change them.
- The therapist may want your entire family in some sessions because he or she may suspect that there are problems in your home that need some attention and could be affecting you.
- If you lie to the therapist, it may feel as if you are protecting yourself, but all you'll be doing is keeping him or her from helping you to help yourself. Things could get worse.
- Your therapist will likely share your private information with your nutritionist. They need to work together.
- You are allowed to get angry at or frustrated with your therapist. This doesn't mean however that she's "the wrong one."
- If you have trouble with things the therapist says or if you don't feel at ease, it could mean that you are not the right match.
- Finally, remind your child that a therapist is not a mind reader. While it is certainly a key responsibility of any therapist to relax a client sufficiently for her to be able to open up, your child still has to be willing to put some information out there.

"The first therapist I went to didn't say a word. She just looked at me. I couldn't stand it. I couldn't wait for the session to be over. I felt trapped and like I wanted to scream, 'If I wasn't crazy before this, I'm going to go crazy now!'"

Warning Signs

Some adolescents may have a bit of difficulty at first with any therapist. Problems do not necessarily mean that your child is resistant or that the therapist is incompetent. It's like any other relationship. Your child will want to feel that it is a good match. But there are some signs that will indicate you need to look more closely at what is going on:

- Your child complains, "We just sit there. No one says a thing." Many therapists believe in a technique that is more watchful and completely nondirective. This is okay for some kids. But many adolescents are more comfortable when someone verbally helps to move them along.
- Your child insists that the therapist "hates me." For reasons you may not completely ever know, your child may feel judged. Perhaps this therapist has a direct way of speaking that leaves your daughter feeling criticized.
- Your child is clearly constantly lying to her therapist. When you call to share a concern with the therapist, he or she seems to have no idea of what you are talking about.

The longer time you insist that your child "stick it out" with a therapist who does not feel right to her, the harder it will be for her to open up enough to find someone with whom she *can* work. Three sessions with a given therapist should be sufficient to tell if there is a connection; however, if your child takes an immediate and intense dislike to a particular therapist (and she is not notably resistant to therapy in general), it is unwise to push her to return even if only one session has taken place. No matter what the circumstance, invite your child to explain why she feels uncomfortable with the therapist, and feel free when checking around for another to inform him or her of your daughter's preferences. "The last professional I took her to made my daughter very uncomfortable. Apparently, she was relentlessly serious in her attitude, and my child was frightened by it."

THE PSYCHIATRIST

Your therapist will likely be the one to inform you if it appears that your child needs to see a psychiatrist. She most certainly will have a few to recommend, as it is common practice for him or her to work with a psychiatrist. While psychiatrists may also serve in the role of therapist, increasingly these doctors concentrate more on the issue of medications that may be warranted to treat clinically significant anxiety or depression. A psychiatrist is trained to make finely tuned assessments of a patient's emotional health and to recommend specific drugs (if necessary) to help attain emotional balance. In most instances of eating disordered behaviors, the need for medication is temporary. The usual course of treatment for depression, anxiety, or obsessive thought is six to twelve months. Initially, the psychiatrist may see the client once every week until he or she is satisfied that the appropriate medication and dosage have been established and that the effect is positive. After the adolescent is stabilized, the psychiatrist may see her at first once a month and then progress to every three months. The psychiatrist stays in close contact with the therapist and nutritionist in order to maintain a full picture of your child's progress both physically and emotionally. At the point at which it is established that medication is no longer required, appointments with the psychiatrist are usually no longer necessary.

During an initial visit with a psychiatrist you might expect questions similar to those asked by a therapist. It's important to have some patience for this process, as the psychiatrist is most probably looking for additional signs and symptoms that would aid him or her in making decisions about medication.

As the psychiatrist's role is similar in some ways to that of a therapist, we are going to condense the following sections a bit. Instead are specific questions or items you will want to consider when choosing a psychiatrist, preparing an adolescent, and watching for warning signs.

How to Choose

Even though a psychiatrist will have regular appointments (in varying intervals) with your child to see how she is faring and to be sure the medications remain appropriate, he or she will not be actively engaging in regular therapy sessions. Still, you will want to make careful decisions. You might want to ask the psychiatrist these questions:

- What is your experience in working with teens who have problems with extreme dieting?
- How do you see the nature of these problems?
- How do you work with other health professionals my child is going to be seeing?
- Under what circumstances do you recommend the use of medications?

How to Prepare an Adolescent

Perhaps the biggest issue your child will face when seeing a psychiatrist is coming to terms with a recommendation that drugs are advisable. Many adolescents fear that this means people will think they are "crazy," "out of control," or going to "change into a whole other person." In fact, you may fear these things as well!

Your child will likely end up in a psychiatrist's office upon the recommendation of her therapist, who is concerned that her emotional problems are serious and that therapy would actually be more effective if your child could get some relief from medication. In order to prepare your child for meeting with a psychiatrist, you need to embrace these ideas:

- Psychiatric drugs are not a crutch. Under acute stress the chemicals in the brain can shift and contribute to depression or anxiety. In other words, there is a real physiological need for drug intervention.
- Personalities don't change with psychotropic medications. However, depression can often be lessened, anxieties relieved, and obsessive thoughts (which frequently accompany eating disordered behaviors) reduced.
- Perfectly sane people often need medications. Perhaps life has been too stressful for too long, or they are genetically predisposed to some emotional difficulties. Neither fact speaks to craziness but rather to vulnerabilities that can be controlled so that they no longer rule the way people think.

It is wise to let your child know that the psychiatrist *may* suggest medications but that no one is going to *force* her to take anything unless it seems necessary. Furthermore, she can and certainly should take some time to consider what is proposed.

> "I really liked Dr. Howard. He was so calm, and he heard every word I said. He was kind of funny too. I told him that I wanted to be a model and that was why I needed to be really thin. I thought he'd give me the rap about how I can't be a model unless I get healthy. Instead he said that maybe I could get started with just head shots. He didn't try and stand in my way. He 'got' what I wanted in life."

Warning Signs

Any time a professional is in a position to prescribe drugs to your child (or you!), it's especially important to stay informed and well aware of any subtle problems. Here are things to watch for:

- The psychiatrist immediately recommends medication without what feels like a thorough clinical evaluation.
- The psychiatrist has a difficult manner in relating to you or your child. Is the psychiatrist gruff, arrogant, or condescending? It doesn't have to be this way!
- There seems to be very minimal follow-through in evaluating the effects of the medications.
- The psychiatrist keeps your child on medications when the response is minimal.
- Your child leaves the session frightened that she might be "nuts."

You will want to find a psychiatrist who is user-friendly—someone who is as connected to patients as to the vast medicine cabinet at his or her disposal. This is, for sure, an inexact science, and any psychiatrist who would lead you to believe that he or she absolutely knows what will work is someone to avoid. What will or won't work can't be known until the psychiatrist gives a particular drug to your particular child. Then, and only then, will the psychiatrist have a pretty good idea of what *seems* to be working.

Clearly there are many professionals out there who are in a position to be tremendously helpful to your child as she combats her an eating disorder. There are many decisions to be made. Which discipline do you go to first? Who is the right person within that field? Does the treatment seem to be one that will work? When should you decide to look further? Many of these questions can be answered by observing your child and following your instincts. You will feel you are in the right place if you perceive that your child is moving forward or, if she is not, that you fully understand what is happening and are being supported by the professionals around you.

The bottom line? You are not alone. Asking for help for a problem that creates conflict between you and your child is a brave and wise thing to do. You are not abdicating to another the responsibility for helping your child with these problems. Your role now will be to work on sharing warm and communicative moments with your child. That is the necessary backdrop to the work that will go on in a professional's office. Without support at home, your child will come home to what might feel to her like a war zone, and any progress made by the professional team will all fall away. It may be hard to step back, but that doesn't mean you are turning away.

Remember, when it comes to the team, *you* are the most important member. It will be a lot easier to do your part if you allow everyone else to do theirs.

nine

The Antidote

Keeping It Healthy

Our children are growing up in a culture that frequently trumpets the idea that it is better to look good than to feel good. It is better to be thin than it is to be healthy and happy. The message has somehow become that to *be* someone you cannot just let yourself be.

Whether you have a child in your house with disordered eating patterns or one who has not yet shown signs of watching her weight in unhealthy ways, it is important to recognize that you do not have to sit back and let the culture just wash over your family. Just as you want to keep your child away from street drugs, it is critical that you keep her off the thinness treadmill. You need to find antidotes.

These antidotes come in many forms. As we touched on throughout, they can be the words or actions you take while sitting quietly at home talking, eating, or watching the television. They may be a conversation with school administrators or coaches. These antidotes are slow-acting measures, of course, but if you stay with them earnestly and with the full weight of your beliefs, there's a better chance that your child will neither move down that slippery slope into an eating disorder nor, if she has yet to diet, begin to do so in an unhealthy fashion.

What follows are our suggestions for creating an atmosphere around your child that promotes more positive feelings about her body and eating and underlines the strength of her entire being—body, mind, and soul.

This chapter represents a compilation of the most important *daily* principles to keep in mind. Some are slightly new takes on what you've already read, but most represent additional thoughts and actions that you will want to remember. There is no guarantee that your child will be able to resist the pressures of the world around her or combat her own inner struggles in a positive way, but what follows represents a large piece of what you, as a parent, might do to help your child maintain her emotional and physical health.

CREATING A HEALTHY SPACE

1. Don't talk about your physical self in a negative way.
Whatever your figure flaw, either keep it to yourself or speak of it as a fact of life—anyone's life—and not a millstone around your neck. If you're in a store with your daughter and she encourages you to try on a pair of pencil-thin slacks, don't say, "Oh, my thighs are way too fat for those pants." Rather, say something like, "Those slacks are not cut well for me. I need a bit more room in the legs." In other words, it's not that you don't fit the clothes. It's that the clothes don't fit you.

Your child has a greater chance of accepting her own body if she sees you not only accept yours but clearly feel good about it. Occasionally you might want to try on a new outfit and say, "I love the way this fits. It's comfortable, and I think it's a great color for me!" It's not that the outfit is slenderizing. It's that the clothing simply enhances who you are. It adds. It doesn't subtract!

2. When describing another person, use words that speak to his or her looks in general terms unrelated to weight.
Many of us have fallen into the easy habit of describing others in terms that emphasize weight—for example, "slender, around 5'5",

red hair, and green eyes." After that we may add almost as an after-thought, "She has a nice smile, she laughs a lot, and she loves her work." Do we really believe that the most important place to start when conjuring up a person is her weight? Think about how often it is that we say, "Well, she's about fifteen pounds overweight, medium height, and has kind of a round face." Too frequently we convey the message that not only is the physical self of greater importance, but we also pinpoint the precise nature of the problem. Even if you spend the next ten minutes describing her smile, her lovely hair, her musi-cal talent, or her intellectual prowess, you will have first and foremost underlined a negative identifying characteristic—fifteen pounds.

As often as possible, begin where you would want your daughter to begin when describing herself. "She has a great personality and sense of humor. She's also really nice. She has blondish hair and blue eyes and is about 5'2"." If possible, avoid the topic of weight altogether. If you daughter asks, "Is she fat?" (and indeed the person you are describing is a bit heavy), shrug and say something like, "Well, she isn't skinny, but fat is a subjective word. What's fat to one person is not fat to another. To me she looks fine."

You will be saying that not only is a person's weight not particu-larly interesting but also that there is no one way to describe it that everyone could agree on.

3. If you hear your child or her friends using disparaging words about someone's weight, stop them.

"She's an elephant." "Thunder thighs." "Moooo." "Fat slob." The possibilities of conjuring up injurious remarks about another person's weight are truly endless. Sadly, these words are uttered most often by adolescents for several reasons: they may feel "fat" themselves; put-ting someone down temporarily alleviates this insecurity; when speaking in a small group, it can be a message of belonging (they're fat, we're not); they may be completely ignorant about the level of disrespect and cruelty they are exhibiting; and they may be experi-encing anxiety (fear of "What if that was me!"). Disparaging remarks about another person's problem can seem to hold it at bay.

It's important that you consider this closely in order to better understand how your child feels before you say anything. "How could you say such mean things?" is a comment your child may not be able to take in, as it completely disregards what's really motivating the remarks. It's also a frontal attack. "I wonder if you realize how hurtful you guys sound" might be a better way to start. "You may not like her," you might acknowledge, "but is it because she's heavy? That's not much of a reason." Phrasing your comments in this nonaccusatory but also interested way will ultimately help your child start to think rather than brush you aside. You might then add, "Most people in this culture who are overweight are pretty self-conscious about it. Why say something that could make them feel worse? If there was something about you that was bothersome, you sure wouldn't want anyone commenting on it!"

Your daughter and her friends may look at you with mild disdain. After all, from their perspective they're just engaging in harmless put-downs. They aren't thinking that they're hurting anyone. They don't even realize that their disparaging remarks may be more in the service of making *themselves* feel better. But at some point, perhaps if the wrong person overhears them or, worse, someone flings an insult in their direction, they will remember your words. With luck, this will empower them to begin to understand what's happened and change the way in which they look at themselves and others.

4. Emphasize your child's interests, inner attributes, and talents.

Even if your child is a real beauty (and especially if she is), keep your eye on her less visible gifts. Emphasize her skills, talents, personality, or interests as often as possible. Compliment her artistic efforts. Be there for her sports events. If she plays an instrument, regardless of her skill level, encourage her to keep at it. "I love having a musician in the family!" "You have the greatest sense of humor!" The point is, *say it!* Then, if she'll let you express why you feel this way, continue: "It's so wonderful the way you really feel the music when you play."

Your child may look away as if it doesn't matter, but it will matter. You will be helping her to stay in touch with her wellspring of inner strengths. This is critical, because when the beauty-conscious world enters her personal sphere and if she doesn't match up as well as she might like, there will be a gentle voice in her head that reminds her of what she does have that's special. It won't necessarily keep her from dieting, but it could go a long way toward her being satisfied with her looks even if they fall short of what she might have ideally loved. After all, she's thin enough. And besides, she's not only smart but a really good flutist!

You are her first mirror. If you reflect back to her a wonderful picture of who she is as a person, that will forever be part of what she sees when she stands before a true reflecting glass.

5. **If your daughter comes home and says "I feel fat,"**
   don't assume that's exactly what she means.

Your impulse might be to say, "Oh honey, you look great!" Or, if she is a bit overweight, "Well, let's see if we can plan a healthy way for you to lose a few pounds." But chances are that feeling fat is not all she feels and may in fact have very little to do with what is really upsetting her. Instead, she may have squeezed a tiny bit of fat at her hips and decided to locate her distress there instead of where it belongs. Teenagers often view the body as something tangible to which to attach a problem. Perhaps she's feeling as if the other kids don't like her very much. There may be a problem at home with either you or a sibling that is getting her down. Is there a lot of pressure on her to do well? Maybe the other girls have all gotten their periods and she hasn't and feels embarrassed and insecure. Truthfully, it could be anything.

The most helpful response to "I feel fat" or, rather, the response that is most likely to help your child express genuine feelings of distress is something like, "I'm sorry you feel that way. It sounds like you're not feeling too good about yourself. What's going on?" Encourage her to talk more generally about whatever it is that is bothering her. It may indeed be that she would like to lose a few pounds, but it is likely more than that. If you center only on the piece of the problem that relates to her weight, you will, in effect, be validating her notion that if she were only thin, everything would be great.

Encouraging her to look inside herself will help her to connect her emotional struggles with her feelings about her body. If she can balance the discomfort between the two, she is far more likely to diet (if she chooses to do so) in a less irrational way.

6. Make sure the coaches at school know how not to set the stage for an eating disorder.

Coaches can play a very important role in a child's life. If sports are important to your child, she will likely invest a great deal in what the coach advises. Unfortunately, too many coaches are uninformed about the symptoms and pervasiveness of eating disorders. They want their athletes to be fit and will often suggest strenuous workouts and specific diets and nutritional plans that can play into an impressionable adolescent's worst fears. Instead of an offhand suggestion, they might hear that unless they do exactly what the coach says—and more—they may end up fat, out of shape, and off the team. So, these children will take the proverbial weight-loss ball and run with it.

You will want to make sure that your child's coach

- Understands the symptoms of a potential eating disorder.
- Strives to educate athletes as to what their bodies need nutritionally.
- Discourages emphasizing weight but rather concentrates on *strength*.
- Discusses the dangers of overexercising.
- Sees the coach's role as extending beyond the sport to promote health and well-being.

7. **If your premenarcheal child is a bit overweight, don't suggest that she diet; trust that she will deal with it when she's a year or two older.**

As we've seen over and over again, our culture and the attendant messages in the media, peer pressure, and more will all surely exert their influence soon enough. She *will* come to realize what the ideal is and where she stands in relation to it. This is anxiety-provoking enough. If you have criticized her in any way by the time she hits the sensitive years, it could send her headlong into unhealthy eating patterns.

If she is eating too many sweets and starches, speak to it from the standpoint of health. "You know, you do eat an awful lot of cookies. They are loaded with sugar. Too much of anything isn't good for you. How about you cut down on the sweets and instead make sure we have those extra big strawberries you love in the house. They have vitamins your body could really use."

Note the substitute. It's a good idea to make it clear that you're not trying to make her stop eating. You just want her to eat foods that are good for her. The message: "Eat! Just eat good stuff!"

8. **Look for early signs of depression, perfectionism, or anxiety.**

Young adolescents often express depression, anxiety, and a quest for perfectionism. It's sometimes easy to just offhandedly observe, "She's going through a moody stage." And in fact the odds are that this is all there is to it. But still, here are some signs that something more entrenched could be developing. She may

- Cry easily.
- Have frequent nightmares.
- Be afraid to try new things, saying "I can't do it."
- Say self-deprecating things such as, "I'm stupid," "I'm terrible at sports," or "No one likes me."
- Erase homework over and over or copy it over several times in an effort to perfect it.

- Have to be the best at everything, or she feels crushed.
- Constantly ask for your approval.

If any of these signs are evident in your child, you make want to seek out professional help. The earlier the depression or anxiety is caught, the better the chance it will not get out of control.

9. Give your child magazines to read or online sites to explore that celebrate a girl's individuality.

You won't be able to stop the constant flow of trendy fashion, Hollywood star, and beauty magazines into the house. Nor should you want to. This is the world your child lives in, and you both need to stay informed—each for your own reasons. Your child wants to make sure she is "with it," and you will want to know what exactly "it" is so that you can help guide her through this maze of false promises and illusions.

Still, there are lesser-known resources that you might want to make sure your daughter sees. There are many sites online that offer brief articles or magazines you can print out that are designed to help young teens respect themselves no matter their strengths and weaknesses. Don't just *tell* your daughter about them, however. *Print some materials out yourself*, put them in a brightly colored folder, and hand them to her. Place them by her bedside. "I thought you'd enjoy this," you might say. "It's about *real* life!" If she asks what you mean, you can simply toss out something like, "I know those magazines you like are fun to read and look at, but do you realize how few people look like the models in the photographs or even live those kinds of lives? Not many." She'll likely shrug, but you can simply say, "I just thought you might like to read something about the real you. It's pretty great."

10. If your daughter is finding that the latest trend in clothes does not fit her, put it in perspective and keep shopping.

Maybe you're shopping with your daughter and, due to her premenarcheal body, it's not an easy time. You can see that she is getting increasingly frustrated and upset. This is in fact one of the first times she's confronted full-throttle frustration with her body. As quickly as possible, you need to put it in perspective for her. This requires a two-pronged approach:

a. Help her understand what is happening to her body. Give her information about the physical changes she's undergoing.
b. Point out that she is still changing and that this is a process her body is now undergoing. Give her reason to hope that this will all change in time.

"You are in the funny stage between being a girl and having the body of a young woman. It's a hard time for many girls your age to find clothes that fit right. It has to be hard for you! But you know, pretty soon, this is all going to be different. As your body matures, your shape will begin to change and in short time more and more clothes will fit. In the meanwhile, if we don't give up I know there are things we could find that will look great. Let's just look at this as your 'travel wardrobe.'"

The idea is to concentrate on the transitional aspect of what she is going through. Remind her regularly that this is all part of normal development. Often, when confronted with a child who is crying that she looks horrible, a parent will be tempted to say, "You don't! You look really good," even if she doesn't quite. Don't go there. Stay away as much as possible from judgment calls on her appearance. Stick with the concept of her developing body as being a natural flow that everyone experiences. It isn't a bad thing. But it can be a bumpy ride.

And remember to take note of this: Your child is certain to notice that a friend is making a far more graceful transition and indignantly cry, "She looks okay. How come I don't?" Don't try to skirt the issue. The truth is not so terrible. "Some people are built in such a way that their body just goes from one stage to another smoothly. I can understand why you think they are lucky. But just give yourself time."

IF SHE IS CURRENTLY BEGINNING
TO EXHIBIT PROBLEM DIETING

The following suggestions are crafted to help you keep your daughter from sliding down that slippery slope into more disordered eating. There are, of course, no guarantees that the development of an eating disorder can be prevented, but the following concepts should help you create an emotional and physical environment that will encourage your daughter to make good decisions.

1. Model healthful eating, minus the "You should do this, too."
Whether your child is dieting or not, or whether you are or not, it is important that you model healthy eating behavior. Eating in moderation several meals a day contributes to a healthy view of how to manage one's nutrition. Occasionally pull out cookbooks and prepare a dish, commenting on how much you enjoy making a meal that tastes great and is good for you.

If you're dieting, do it sensibly and don't comment on it. If your child sees you eating a platter of low-fat cottage cheese surrounded by blueberries and strawberries, the message will be, "Even if I need to diet, I like to eat. It's nice to diet without feeling deprived."

Avoid, however, "Try this!" or "See how I eat?!" If it becomes a lesson, she won't learn a thing except to stay away from you when you are eating. If she is allowed to merely observe, you'll be giving her the room she needs to decide for herself. That is developmentally the right place for her to be.

2. Accept the limits of your power.
Ultimately, an adolescent with eating behaviors that are becoming disordered is going to have to decide for herself how she is going to address this struggle. The more you push, the more likely she will resist, which is how it often is when dealing with adolescents. In fact, the more you seek to control what and when she eats, the more you will convey a potentially destructive message: "I don't think you

have any idea what you're doing. Nor do I think you have the wisdom to help yourself."

This is precisely what you *do not* want to convey. It is important to let your child know that you believe her capable of making good decisions. The process of taking her to a nutritionist or therapist does not have to undermine this message, either. "I believe you can make some smart choices, but I have a feeling you're feeling stuck and need some help. That's why I'd like you to see someone."

Unless the particular therapist charges you with a responsibility to monitor your child in some way, it is best to conduct mealtimes as normally as possible. Of course, this would involve planning meals to include foods that your child is likely to eat. Cooking low-fat foods such as steamed fresh vegetables and broiled fish or chicken is good for everyone! But if you want a potato, make enough for everybody. It's the family meal, after all. Just as you have limited power, so should your child's eating disorder. It shouldn't completely dictate the menu.

3. Exercise together in social, not emotionally charged, ways.
Many adolescents undertake strenuous exercise as a means to lose weight. Self-reporting reveals that they religiously count the minutes they're on each machine, the flights of stairs they run up and down, or the sit-ups and weights they use to the point that pleasure in exercise and being active is completely lost. It's nothing but a brutal dietary supplement. Your children need to view exercise as more than just that. It's something that if done healthfully can lift moods, provide an atmosphere for socializing, and at the same time keep their bodies in good physical shape. When you go off to exercise, either for a speed walk with a friend or to the gym, be careful about such comments as "I need to do this after that meal I ate last night!" Try instead, "Jane and I are going to get some exercise and finally grab some time to talk!"

Whenever possible, invite your daughter to take a walk, saying, "It's good for the heart and lungs! Besides, we can catch up a little on how the school play [or whatever school activity your child is participating in] is going." The idea here? A person's body is not just about what it looks like from the outside. Exercise is good for what makes it tick, and so is socializing.

4. Model talking about feelings.

Depression can set in when negative feelings go unexpressed. It isn't that anyone *enjoys* not talking about how they feel. Unhappy people may not even understand themselves what is truly causing their emotional pain. Then, too, if they do have an idea of where the problem lies, they may be too afraid to talk for fear of not being understood. They might be laughed at, their words may be interpreted differently than they are meant, they may incur someone's anger, or they might simply be dismissed. Far better, it would seem, to keep difficult emotions inside.

It is important to model emotional language for your child as often as possible. If someone upsets you and it's not highly personal or inappropriate, talk about it, expressing how you felt. Use words such as "embarrassed," "hurt," "angry," "betrayed," etc. Help to build her emotional vocabulary. If she has the words available to her, she just might use them.

Another communication issue to consider is the raised voice. There are many households in which people tread extremely carefully with each other. Raised voices, or out-and-out yelling, just never happens. To be sure, it would seem to make for a calm and respectful atmosphere. But an occasional blowup is not such a bad thing either. It teaches a child that people can get really angry, express their feelings truthfully, and still love each other. If there is a constant low ebb of emotions, your child may feel constricted and turn inward. This can lead to a search for relief—such as dieting.

It is very important for our children to understand that anger does not have to annihilate anyone. They and you can survive a battle and come out the stronger for it.

5. If you notice a surge in dieting or a sudden binge, talk about her feelings, not her body.

You walk into the kitchen and find your daughter standing in front of the counter, upon which rests a newly purchased half-eaten bag of cookies, a tall glass of chocolate milk, and the leftover lasagna. She's been dieting quite seriously, and just the other day you urged her to let up a little, noting that she looked thin enough. She had merely shrugged. This scene in the kitchen, however, is equally unsettling. Part of you wants to simply say, "What are you doing?!"

The fact is, if you just pause and take this in, you will see precisely what she's doing. You don't need to ask. She's bingeing because she's very hungry. And she's likely to be quite anxious as well. A person doesn't go from serious dieting to binge eating without a sense that things have slipped beyond their control. The issue is *not* what she is doing but rather what she is feeling. Why has she been dieting so stringently? Is she really this hungry, or is she really more anxious than anything else? How does she feel standing there doing this? Would she like someone to help her?

"Wow," you might say in a sympathetic tone, "you sure look like something is up with you. Are you okay?" In other words, don't comment directly about the food. Stick with what might be behind her actions. Let your daughter know that you realize there's more going on than a foodfest. Of course, even she may not know that. But if you don't point it out, she'll have a lot more trouble getting there. If she asks what you mean, be direct. "Well, first you were dieting a lot. Now you're suddenly going at the food, and I'm wondering if something is on your mind. Usually when people do things in extremes it's because they are feeling very upset and overwhelmed."

If she insists that nothing is wrong or bothering her, you might want to say, "I don't want you to end up feeling sick. How about we put the rest of this away, and in a bit we can talk." Say this calmly. You want your message to transmit the idea that you don't want to tell her what to do, but on the other hand you are concerned for her and want her to feel well in all ways. This approach will likely lessen the anxiety she is feeling (not to mention shame and embarrassment), and she may very well be able to put away the food, probably with a fair amount of relief.

6. **If you have a disagreement with your adolescent about anything that is not life-threatening, state your case but be sure to empower your child.**

As discussed several times in this book, there is a control issue behind strenuous dieting and eating disorders. For many sufferers it is a way to feel in charge when they actually feel powerless. Either life is just too difficult or no one is listening to how they are feeling, or both, and in general they experience themselves as victimized. Dieting is a way of saying, "I am now the one in control of me."

The question, then, is how do you create an environment in which you are still in charge but your child does not feel as if she has no power at all? You do this by genuinely recognizing that she needs to express herself and that you will be a concerned and attentive listener. You do this by recognizing and acknowledging that not *every* time you feel strongly about something you are being fair or that you are even right. You do this by clearly respecting her enough to say, "Okay. I don't like this. But you are a smart and capable girl. Tell me what you're thinking and let's see if there is any room to compromise." An adolescent who is not regularly told "Because I say so" when she disagrees with a parent but instead is invited to have input will experience herself as being valued, having choices, and retaining some control over what happens to her. This will translate into a child who doesn't need to find symbolic ways to gain power. She will literally have some power, and it will go a long way toward her expressing her needs in a straightforward, honest way. She won't need to diet to the brink of an eating disorder to achieve a sense of "I am the master of my own life."

She won't even need to be the master, because in truth a child who is listened to and respected and understood secretly welcomes a boundary or two.

7. Don't keep checking up on her.

There is an obsessive aspect to eating disordered behaviors. And it's contagious. As often as your daughter wonders,

> "Have I put on an ounce?"
> "Should I eat this?"
> "Does my butt look fat?"

you might be thinking,

> "Did she eat her bagel or throw it out on the way to school?"
> "Should I call someone at the cafeteria to make sure she eats?"
> "What can I cook that she'll eat?"

You may be tempted and even feel driven to ask,

> "Did you eat today?"
> "Did you get a snack?"
> "Have you checked to see if you're still losing?"

In short, you can each drive yourselves crazy. Not to mention each other.

Understand that no matter what you hear, you will not readily be comforted. If she answers "Yes" you'll be relieved for five minutes and then wonder the rest of the evening if she's lying. If she answers "No" you'll worry all evening that things are spinning seriously out of control. Either way, you remain uncertain and worried.

The only thing that really matters is what she is *actually* doing. Constantly checking is not likely to change her behavior for the better; it might even upset her enough to worsen the symptoms. She'll feel as if she has the proverbial monkey on her back, and instead of the monkey being the eating disorder, it will be you. Or, perhaps worse, there will be two monkeys chattering in her ear, each at times with opposing messages. "Eat." "Don't eat." "Eat." "Don't Eat."

Ultimately, your daughter is going to have to struggle and then make up her own mind. No amount of checking and double checking on your part is going to in any way help her do that.

Checking *can* make you feel as if you're keeping on top of things. You aren't. You are merely burying yourself and your daughter with your own anxieties.

8. When you and your spouse don't agree.

Frequently parents do not agree on whether or not there is a problem, and if they do agree they can be quite critical of the way in which the other chooses to handle it. This is an arena where each person's basic views on parenting or working through a crisis can emerge. You may believe it's important to pounce the minute you see a problem so that things don't worsen. Your husband may feel that first one needs to give a problem time to work itself out. You may feel that a person needs to pull him or herself up by the boot-straps, and anything short of this is weak. Your husband may feel that this is an impossibly demanding expectation and that most people need help with their emotional problems.

A problem with your child can also tap into other issues in your relationship. At times, serious rifts in the marriage can erupt as the child is flirting with an eating disorder. Perhaps you feel that your husband not only doesn't notice how distressed your daughter is but also that he rarely notices when *you* are feeling stressed or exhausted. He may view you as hopelessly controlling not only of what your daughter does but also in the way that you place expectations on him. You may begin to argue not only about your daughter but also the way you are with each other.

It is fair to say that any serious problem in a family can shed a spotlight on all other interpersonal weaknesses and that, as a result, things can begin to implode. This can also actually drive a child who is flirting with a disorder more quickly down that slippery slope.

There is really only one clear option here. For your child's sake and the well-being of all family members, it is important to seek family consultation. Many people try to bypass this, fearing that once in the therapist's office they will be blamed for the family woes. But well-trained therapists do not engage in finger-pointing. For the most part, they view families as *systems*. This means that each of you is seen as playing a vital role in your functioning unit, and everyone plays a part in what throws it off kilter. Cracks in the system, some of which may have existed for some time, now show up. The situation is complicated. Certainly the initial visible problem has to be addressed, but in order for it not to continue or reappear, the other strains in family ties have to be dealt with as well. Only then will an equilibrium return.

In other words, the objective of family therapy is not to find the culprit. The objective is to look at the manner in which you interact with each other, both the positives and the negatives, and find the means to correct the weaknesses and build on the strengths. Everyone is responsible for that.

9. The disordered eating behaviors should not be allowed to throw the household into disorder.

If your child has reached stage three of the slippery slope, there can be a number of practical problems that arise from her largely chaotic dieting and eating patterns. You will want to try to find solutions and give her some responsibility for the ramifications of what she does, but not so much as to increase her symptoms.

If your daughter occasionally binges, do you keep all binge type foods out of the house? Or, what if you wake up one morning and most of the food that was in the refrigerator last night has been eaten?

The truth is that if your child wants to binge, she will do it whether she is home or not. While it certainly may be wise not to keep the cabinets filled with cookies and chips, if there are family members who enjoy such snacks in moderation, they should be kept available. Ultimately your daughter has to make the decision herself as to what to eat. If she empties the shelves, you might want to decide to give her some responsibility for that. Either she needs to do the shopping to replace the food or perhaps have some money taken out of her allowance to contribute to replacements.

If your daughter has purged (even though it is very infrequent) along with her dieting and leaves the bathroom in something of a mess, who should clean it? The fact is that she should take responsibility for her actions. It needn't be done in a punishing way. Simply provide what she should need under the sink, make your point, and leave it to her. By helping your daughter take responsibility for her actions, you will be helping her toward a sense of responsibility both to herself and others.

What if the household chores include small jobs around meal-time? If the jobs are to be evenly shared, should your daughter be asked to participate in meal preparation or cleanup? Ofttimes siblings of a child who is flirting with an eating disorder resent that their sister is not made to do chores surrounding food, such as washing the dishes. A sense of injustice or resentment is not a healthy family dynamic. Still, to push your daughter in an arena where she clearly has problems could drive her to more erratic behaviors. It might be wise to give her responsibilities that are less stressful to her. Perhaps she can do the family laundry once a week, or if you have a den or family room, she could be the one to neaten it up every night before the family goes to sleep.

Making decisions about what you should or shouldn't ask your child to do can be unnerving—you're likely going to be uncertain about the right approach. Professional consultation will be crucial here in helping you find the right balance between exercising your responsibility as a parent and giving your child her necessary share of responsibility in managing her own behavior.

10. Stay away from blame.
"If only I had . . ."

When strung together these are four useless and misguided words. Not that what you *might* have done definitely wouldn't have mattered, but there is absolutely no proof that had you gone another route, things would have turned out better or even differently.

It's easy to look at things that you or other members of your family might have done to set the stage for the problem your child is now having. But it is critical to remember that many factors have been at play, and what matters now is how to help your child move forward in a positive, healthy way.

No matter what you fervently wish you had or hadn't done, we believe it is highly likely that it wouldn't have been enough to stand between your daughter and her flirtation with an eating disorder. Things are just not that simple.

The next time you feel yourself moving toward self-flagellation, remind yourself of these three things:

- Some of the same roads that lead to eating disorders also don't.
- The development of an eating disorder depends also on a child's unique sensitivities.
- The person on the path is affected by you but ultimately makes her own decisions based on her world. Her world includes you but is not completely defined by you.

In other words, it's fair to say that you may have your role in the problems your child might have, but whatever your weaknesses, whatever your mistakes, they did not necessarily have to lead directly to unhealthy dieting. Your child brings her own self to the task of managing life.

Rather than pouring your energy into blame, preserve your strengths for helping your child cope and recover.

ten
‾‾‾

A Brief Look at Some
Relevant Research

We hope this book has helped you see your child's dieting behaviors within a context that is neither frightening nor hopeless but, in fact, manageable, and if not commonplace at least common enough.

So often we hear parents express embarrassment, fear, or shame. They feel that they are spectacularly alone and lacking in successful parenting skills. They believe themselves to be members of such a tiny minority that their child's eating disordered behaviors take on an almost freakish aspect.

This sense of being "bizarre" and "the only ones" is not only incorrect (and harsh) but potentially damaging to your own capacity to deal constructively with the problem at hand. What we've tried to do in this book is help you minimize the internal struggle you may experience. There is one final piece to our efforts.

This chapter will introduce some research that explores common questions about eating disorders as they manifest in the general population. Throughout this book you have found information and suggestions for helping your child. The intent of this chapter is to help you place the problems of eating disordered behaviors in context. You need to see that you are experiencing something many parents face and recognize that the troubles your child may have are, to one degree or another, well documented and faced by others her age.

Many research studies show that a large proportion of teens believe that they are too heavy, and upwards of 60 percent diet.[1] So, the mere fact that your child is dissatisfied with her appearance and wishes to shed some pounds is hardly unusual.

If your child is dieting in a way that is of concern, her behavior regarding food has come about for a variety of reasons. A better understanding of these reasons will help you aid her in the most constructive ways possible.

HOW COMMON ARE PROBLEM DIETING BEHAVIORS?

"I am so embarrassed that my daughter clearly has some kind of an eating disorder. I mean, I've already gotten two calls from concerned parents—as if I haven't noticed. I feel like a freak."

Uncomfortable as this parent is, the fact is that dieting behaviors are quite common among teens. Still, there are good reasons for at least raising the question of whether or not those behaviors can progress to an eating disorder. Eating disorders are recognized widely as a public health issue of immense importance, and their beginning stages take the form of the same behaviors that compose the slippery slope. So, early recognition of the risk factors for more serious problems is crucial for effective early intervention.

1. M. K. Serdula, M. E. Collins, D. F. Williamson, et al., Weight control practices of U.S. adolescents and adults, *Annals of Internal Medicine* 119 (1993): 667; A. B. Middleman, I. Vazquez, and R. H. Durant, Eating patterns, physical activity, and attempts to change weight among adolescents, *Journal of Adolescent Health* 22 (1998): 37; D. P. Krowchuk, S. R. Kreiter, C. R. Woods, et al., Problem dieting behaviors among young adolescents, *Archives of Pediatric Medicine* 152 (1998): 884; S. A. French, C. L. Perry, G. R. Leon, et al., Dieting behaviors and weight change history in female adolescents, *Health Psychology* 14 (1995): 548.

Extreme methods at weight control such as prolonged fasting, vomiting, and use of laxatives or diet pills are surprisingly common, as indicated by upwards of 13 percent of female teens in anonymous surveys. Furthermore, these potentially dangerous behaviors tend to go together and are often associated with poor school functioning. For example, a research study conducted by Daniel Krowchuk found that girls who used diet pills were much more likely to also induce vomiting or use laxatives compared to teens who never used diet pills and that girls with poor academic functioning were much more likely to report using these high-risk weight control behaviors.[2] In this sample, nearly 25 percent considered themselves overweight, 40 percent were trying to lose weight, and 22 percent were trying to keep the same weight. The most common measures used to lose or maintain weight included exercise (59.4 percent), dieting (34 percent), vomiting or taking laxatives (9.4 percent), and taking diet pills (6.7 percent). Academic status was related to eating habits. Girls who considered themselves "best students" were 1.2 times more likely to have vomited or used laxatives, while girls who rated themselves at the bottom of their class were 7.4 times more likely to have used such risky weight-loss techniques. In other words, very poor school performance seems to go hand in hand with more dangerous weight-loss behaviors.

A study conducted at the University of Minnesota looked at the prevalence of very frequent dieting through adolescence, defined as being on a diet more than ten times in the previous year.[3] This study revealed that such efforts increase steadily with age in girls: 7.8 percent for seventh and eight graders, 13.5 percent for ninth and tenth graders, and 14.3 percent for eleventh and twelfth graders. Among boys, the prevalence of such dieting was lower, only 1.6 percent, 2.5 percent and 2.4 percent, respectively.

2. D. P. Krowchuk, S. R. Kreiter, C. R. Woods, et al., Problem dieting behaviors among young adolescents, *Archives of Pediatric Medicine* 152 (1998): 884–888.

3. M. Story et al., Demographic and risk factors associated with chronic dieting in adolescents, *American Journal of Diseases in Childhood* 145 (1991): 994.

Clearly, the use of risky weight-loss behaviors by adolescents deserves our attention and concern. What is especially worrisome about this is that these behaviors can be associated with the later development of eating disorders. These studies demonstrate the importance of being alert to the beginning signs of more extreme dieting and any indication of dangerous weight-loss strategies whose presence can increase the risk of eating disorder.

IS IT INEVITABLE IN THIS CULTURE THAT MY DAUGHTER WILL HAVE TROUBLE WITH HER BODY IMAGE?

"I listened to my daughter the other day go through the details of her body as if it were nothing but a collection of unsatisfactory pieces. Her thighs, her waist, her upper arms. I was waiting for her to complain about her big toe."

If body dissatisfaction and dieting are so common among teens in our culture, what separates this majority from those who eventually develop more serious extremes of dieting and weight-loss behaviors? An excellent summary of this research has been conducted by Eric Stice of the University of Texas.[4] We draw from his review to highlight the significant findings.

First, let's look at what we know about the emergence of body dissatisfaction during early adolescence. Increasing our knowledge about the factors that contribute to more extreme dissatisfaction is crucial, because this self-criticism has been linked by some researchers to emotional distress, low self-esteem, depression, and later eating disorders.[5]

We can't stress enough that dissatisfaction with appearance is tied closely to our social world. In recent decades, the pressure on

4. E. Stice, Risk and maintenance factors for eating pathology: A meta-analytic review, *Psychological Bulletin* 128 (2002): 825.
5. J. Killen et al., Weight concerns influence the development of eating disorders, *Journal of Clinical and Consulting Psychology* 64 (1996): 936.

young people, girls in particular, to achieve thinness and to see the success of doing so as equal to other accomplishments has intensified. The message is conveyed through the media, peer pressure, parental encouragement, and more, making it virtually impossible to avoid as it permeates every aspect of our daily routine.

A variety of factors can increase body image dissatisfaction at the time of puberty. These include an early start of menstruation, a higher than average body mass, being teased for excessive weight, depression, overvaluation of thinness, and lack of adequate social support. Eric Stice and his colleagues tested these effects in a longitudinal study of nearly five hundred girls who ranged in age from 11 to 15.[6] The girls were interviewed, had their height and weight measured, and filled out questionnaires tapping into factors thought to be related to body image. The girls were then interviewed again a year later in order to isolate factors that predicted an increase in their body dissatisfaction.

Two variables predicted an increase in dissatisfaction over time: higher weight and the perceived pressure to be thin. The researchers further determined that perceived pressure to be thin was the most powerful predictor of body dissatisfaction. Girls who reported that they felt at least "a little pressure to be thin" were at four times greater risk for developing body dissatisfaction than girls who reported only a little pressure to be thin. Stice also found that among girls who reported low pressure to be thin, those whose weight was above the average were at eight times greater risk for onset of body dissatisfaction compared to those with lower weight. Other findings showed that a lack of strong social supports also predicted body dissatisfaction. The researchers concluded that body dissatisfaction arises in part because female adolescents "cannot achieve the level of thinness promoted in Western cultures but that acceptance within one's social network might help girls feel more

6. E. Stice, Risk factors for body dissatisfaction in adolescent girls: A longitudinal investigation, *Developmental Psychology* 38 (2002): 669.

secure about themselves and their bodies," thus leaving them less vulnerable to sociocultural pressure to be thin.[7]

So, as common as body dissatisfaction is among teens, it appears to vary in intensity and is promoted by various physical, social, and emotional factors.

BODY IMAGE, EATING PROBLEMS, AND EMOTIONAL DISORDERS

"My daughter is not happy with her body type. I keep telling her everyone is different and she shouldn't keep tearing herself apart. She has a nice athletic build. Still, it seems to be she's getting more and more disgusted with herself and is more self-critical."

"I hate my body!"

All too many parents hear this sentiment out of the mouths of their adolescent daughters. It is uttered with varying degrees of conviction to be sure, but it does speak to dramatic and potentially negative emotions. Often your daughter will be at great odds with her body—the way in which it compares to what she thinks it ought to be. If the difference between what it is and what she wants it to be is too vast, this could set the stage for extreme self-doubt or depression.

Early on in this book we touched on the question of what comes first. Do emotional problems cause body hatred and a subsequent eating disorder, or does body dissatisfaction, born of many different factors, result in emotional problems that can then lead to an eating disorder? Well, the connections run in both directions.

Before we consider the role of emotional disturbance per se, it is important to look at the role that personality traits play in the development of an eating disorder. Attempts have been made to investigate the backgrounds of people with anorexia nervosa and

7. Ibid., 676.

bulimia nervosa in order to isolate personal vulnerabilities that could lead to these disorders. Anorexia nervosa is a serious illness associated with extreme fear of normal body weight. The dieting of people with anorexia nervosa results not only in weight loss but also in dangerous malnutrition that can retard growth and cause serious bone disease. Roughly 5–6 percent of those who fall ill will die from the effects of prolonged emaciation. Bulimia nervosa, on the other hand, may also arise as a consequence of efforts at dieting, but there is no emaciation; rather, the person develops uncontrolled eating binges in which painfully large amounts of food are consumed, followed by efforts to eliminate the calories taken in by self-induced vomiting or use of laxatives.

Christopher Fairburn and colleagues at Oxford University in England investigated an extensive array of risk factors believed to play a role in eating disorders.[8] They interviewed 67 females with anorexia nervosa, 102 with bulimia nervosa, 102 with other types of psychiatric disturbance, and 204 with no emotional or eating disturbance. For anorexia nervosa, a background of low self-regard and extreme perfectionism stood out most dramatically. As for bulimia, the background factors of greatest importance were criticism of appearance, parental obesity and elevated body weight, and exposure to family emotional turmoil. Other findings in the research literature that are consistent with these results include extensive documentation of personality traits such as extreme rigidity, perfectionism, and inhibition associated with anorexia nervosa, along with very high rates of childhood anxiety in both anorexia and bulimia nervosa.[9] Thus, insecurity, self-doubt, extreme perfectionism, and rigidity of

8. C. Fairburn, Z. Cooper, H. A. Doll, et al., Risk factors for anorexia nervosa: Three integrated case-control comparisons, *Archives of General Psychiatry* 56 (1999): 468.

9. C. Bulik et al., Eating disorders and antecedent anxiety disorders: A controlled study, *Acta Psychiatrica Scandanavica* 96 (1997): 101; K. Klump, C. M. Bulik, C. Pollice, et al., Temperament and character in women with anorexia nervosa, *Journal of Nervous and Mental Disease* 188 (2000): 559.

personality, along with a tendency to develop fears to a far greater extent than is average, may underlie at least part of the vulnerability to severe eating disorders.

There have been other attempts to link eating disorders to psychological disturbance generally. These findings are important to highlight because they can alert you and health professionals to the risks associated with persistent or extreme dieting when such problems are in the teen's personal or family history.

As noted, elevated body weight, body dissatisfaction, and dieting are common in girls at the time of puberty. What is less than clear is whether these factors are a cause or a consequence of depression in young people. The psychologist Eric Stice and colleagues sought to determine whether body image and eating-related factors such as dieting and bulimic pathology arise before or are effects of depression in teens. Specifically, the researchers assessed "whether elevation in body mass, body dissatisfaction, dieting and bulimic symptoms predicted onset of major depression among initially non-depressed adolescent girls."[10]

The 1,124 participants in the study were female students ranging in age from 13 years to 16 years, 9 months. At the time they entered the study and during three annual follow-up assessments, each female adolescent had her weight and height measured and participated in a structured interview. An estimate of body fat was obtained, and questionnaires were used to assess depressive symptoms, body dissatisfaction, dietary restraint behaviors, and bulimic symptoms.

Stice and his colleagues found that higher initial levels of body dissatisfaction, dietary restraint, and bulimic symptoms predicted greater risk for later onset of depression, but higher body fat did not. In other words, it was not the actual weight but the *perceived* weight

10. E. Stice et al., Body-image and eating disturbances predict onset of depression among female adolescents: A longitudinal study, *Journal of Abnormal Psychology* 109 (2000): 438.

that was an issue. The researchers interpreted the results to mean that extreme dieting resulted from body dissatisfaction, which then leads to increasing depression because of the high rate of failure associated with dieting. Lastly, bulimic symptoms were also found to predict depression, suggesting that the shame, guilt, and social impact associated with binge eating and purging can result in depressed mood.

Another study that explored the effects of psychiatric problems on later risk of eating disorders was published in 2002 by researchers at Columbia University.[11] These researchers performed diagnostic assessments on more than 700 youths in 1983 and reinterviewed the sample in 1985, and then again between 1991 and 1993. The most important finding was that a diagnosis of depression in 1983 was associated with a higher risk of later eating disorder. But the specific aspects of depression that might be increasing the risk of a later eating disorder (e.g., depression is believed to have social, emotional, and biological causes) remain uncertain.

Clearly, then, whereas the social, physical, and emotional impact of an eating disorder can give rise to depression, there is also evidence that mood- and anxiety-related problems can increase the risk of developing eating disorders.

IS AN EATING DISORDER INEVITABLE IF SHE DOESN'T LIKE HER BODY?

"Do I need to start worrying the minute she goes on a diet and starts working out to get rid of the 'fat'? I mean, I dieted when I was a kid, too. So did my friends. We didn't get sick though."

Naturally, not every adolescent who wishes that her body looked different is going to develop unhealthy eating patterns. We already

11. J. G. Johnson, P. Cohen, L. Kotler, et al., Psychiatric disorders associated with risk for the development of eating disorders during adolescence and early adulthood, *Journal of Consulting and Clinical Psychology* 70 (2002): 1119.

noted that the prevalence of severe eating disorders is far less than dieting behavior in general. Still, it stands to reason that as dissatisfaction with one's body rises, so does the possibility of restrictive dieting. As you have seen in earlier chapters, much depends on the way in which an adolescent interacts with the environment as well as on her personality traits, social circles, family dynamics, and general sense of self. You may feel baffled by your daughter's distorted eating behaviors because when you were a teen, most kids dieted in a more controlled fashion. Of course, you grew up in a world of body-consciousness too, but it would appear that today the glories of thinness reach untold proportions.

Various research studies show that elevated levels of dissatisfaction do, in fact, increase the risk of more extreme dieting and that elevations in dieting behavior similarly elevate the risk of later disordered eating, more disturbed eating attitudes, and risk of binge eating and related bulimic symptoms. However, these relationships are by no means straightforward.

The work of Eric Stice has shown these associations. In a study appearing in 2002, the researchers evaluated more than 200 females, 13 to 17 years of age at the time of initial assessment, and then retested the subjects at ten months and again at twenty months after initial assessment.[12] At least one episode of binge eating occurred in 13–14 percent of the sample at each assessment point. Risk of developing binge eating over time, if it wasn't present at initial assessment, was predicted by an increased frequency of dieting behaviors, elevated body weight, overvaluation of thinness, perception of greater pressure to be thin, and exposure to disordered eating behavior in peers, parents, or the media.

Some further examination of the data gave additional insight into exactly who is at risk. For girls who did not place excess importance on appearance, only depressed mood increased the risk of

12. E. Stice et al., Risk factors for binge eating onset: A prospective investigation, *Health Psychology* 21 (2002): 131.

developing binge eating. By contrast, if girls placed a high value on thinness, the risk of binge eating was greater when girls with higher body weight dieted. A reasonable general interpretation of these findings is that as body weight increases, so does the tendency for teens to experience dissatisfaction with appearance and to diet—but mainly when the perceived pressure to be thin is great and if the teen believes that it is very important to be thin. Interestingly, higher body weight itself does not appear to promote disordered eating; it does so only when these other factors are present.

So, what we can see here is that multiple factors, rather than any single issue, combine in promoting risk for disordered eating. No single factor is itself powerful enough to create the risk. For some depression is key, whereas for others a heightened sensitivity to the message that being thin is of crucial psychological importance seems to promote body dissatisfaction, especially when weight is greater than average. The person tries to resolve her concern through extreme dieting, thus increasing the risk of binge eating.

CAN PEER PRESSURE INSPIRE MY CHILD TO DIET TOO MUCH?

"Every time I told my child that she seemed to be losing a lot of weight, I would hear, 'You should see my friends!' I couldn't decide if that meant they were losing weight at a faster rate or she was trying to say she's just like everyone else. I would reply that I don't care about them, I only care about you, to which she would give me a look that said, 'Yeah? Well you try being me.' Or at least that's what it felt like."

Much research indicates that adolescent friends tend to have similar sets of characteristics, including attitudes and behaviors, physical and social attributes, and especially health-risk behaviors such as smoking and drinking. Might groups of adolescents also share similar body image concerns and eating behaviors that serve as direct models for dieting behaviors? In an Australian study, Susan Paxton and colleagues examined aspects of friendship cliques that may influence body image and eating attitudes.[13] Their study hypothesized that some characteristics such as body concern, dietary restraint, binge eating, and use of extreme weight-loss behaviors would be associated with other influences such as weight-related talk with peers, peer teasing, peer pressure to be thin, and body comparison. The 523 female participants were drawn from the tenth grade and represented a wide range of geographic and social classes.

Results indicated that friendship cliques shared similar levels of dietary restraint, extreme weight-loss behaviors, and levels of body image concern. The findings also suggested that the groups of female friends who exhibited higher levels of body image concern and weight-loss behaviors also reported talking more about weight loss and dieting, compared their bodies often, were concerned with dieting, and perceived their friends as being preoccupied with diet and weight loss. Perhaps, then, an adolescent's perception of her friend's attitudes and actions relating to body image and dieting could affect her own level of body dissatisfaction and need for dieting. The authors conclude that girls can model the behaviors and attitudes of their peers and adopt these as normal. But they also caution that because girls have different peer groups, the nature of adolescent friendships is not so clearly defined as to say that girls only associate with those of similar body concerns.

DO GENES MATTER?

"I went through a stage where I dieted too much as a teenager. I'm still very thin. Sometimes I skip a meal. I guess she got this from me?"

13. S. Paxton et al., Friendship clique and peer influences on body image concerns, dietary restraint, extreme weight-loss behaviors, and binge eating in adolescent girls, *Journal of Abnormal Psychology* 108 (1999): 255.

The answer to the question "Did she get it from me?" is certainly a complicated one. However, studies do offer evidence supporting the idea that adolescents are more likely to develop partial or full eating disorders if relatives have suffered from the illness. Genetic predisposition may be part of the explanation as to why only some teens spiral into clearly pathological extremes of weight loss and chaotic eating.

One line of evidence has come from family studies that consider whether or not an illness is more common in biological relatives of people with illness compared to relatives of never-ill controls. In my role as director of the Eating Disorders Program at the UCLA Neuropsychiatric Institute, I conducted the largest study to date examining this question.[14]

Groups of women ranging in ages from 18 to 28 years were used in the study. The first group consisted of 152 participants with pure anorexia nervosa. The second group was comprised of 171 participants with pure bulimia nervosa. The third group consisted of 181 participants without any psychiatric illnesses. The relatives of each group were assessed for various psychiatric disorders, including eating disorders.

It was found that 94 women relatives from the three groups were diagnosed as having full or partial eating disorders, and 85 of these women were relatives of subjects with eating disorders. Specifically, a history of anorexia nervosa was eleven times greater in relatives of subjects with anorexia nervosa compared to relatives of the comparison group, and relatives of participants with bulimia nervosa had a rate of bulimia nervosa four times as high as the rate in relatives of the never-ill comparison group. The findings suggest that families can in some way transmit a risk of eating disorders across generations.

But relatives have in common both environments and genes. So how do we know, then, if it is heredity or environment that causes

14. M. Strober, R. Freeman, C. Lampert, et al., Controlled family study of anorexia nervosa and bulimia nervosa: Evidence of shared liability and transmission of partial syndromes, *American Journal of Psychiatry* 157 (2000): 393.

eating disorders to run in families? To address this question, researchers have studied eating disorders in twins. Since identical twins share all of their genes in common, as opposed to fraternal or nonidentical twins who share half, a much greater risk of the same disorder in each of two identical twins compared to nonidentical twins would point to a role for genetic factors.

Studies of twins are few in number, but available research indicates that genetic factors influence the risk of developing both anorexia nervosa and bulimia nervosa.[15] Interestingly, other twin studies also suggest that individual symptoms of disordered eating such as dietary restraint, vomiting and binge eating, extreme body dissatisfaction, and eating and weight concerns are also influenced, at least partly, by genetic factors. However, no specific genes influencing disordered eating behavior have been identified thus far. Researchers are continuing the search.

SO, WHAT ARE THE CHANCES MY DIETING CHILD COULD ACTUALLY BECOME ANOREXIC, AND CAN IT BE PREVENTED?

In reality, very, very few teens who start to lose weight as a result of dieting will develop anorexia nervosa. We know that less than .5 percent of girls develop the illness. And as we showed above, the ones at greatest risk are those who exhibit an extremely rigid personality with extreme perfectionism and who are self-doubting, anxious, and uncomfortable with change. And even when these traits are present, it should not be assumed that anorexia nervosa is inevitable, only that there is greater reason to be more careful in monitoring your child's situation.

15. K. Klump, W. Kaye, and M. Strober, The evolving genetic foundation of eating disorders, *Psychiatric Clinics of North America* 24 (2001): 215; C. M. Bulik, P. F. Sullivan, T. Wade, et al., Twin studies of eating disorders: A review, *International Journal of Eating Disorders* 27 (2000): 1.

In my role at the UCLA Neuropsychiatric Institute I naturally view the goal of prevention as a noble one—the public health implications are enormous. Just the same, the challenges involved are daunting. The task would be less difficult if eating disorders had simple, single causes, but we know this isn't so. Developmental, social, and biological factors are all present, combining in ways that are not yet fully understood. Furthermore, this mix is likely to vary unpredictably from person to person. Yet another major hurdle is the relative infrequency of severe eating disorders in the population. From the standpoint of research statistics, it is difficult to demonstrate that a specific intervention can actually prevent a rare condition from occurring unless very large samples are studied under rigorous experimental conditions. But the cost in research dollars of such an effort would be prohibitive, and the hurdle of mounting a long-term study of this type would be enormous.

Still, efforts have been undertaken to demonstrate that school-based programs can reduce the likelihood of teens initiating certain behaviors that have been implicated in eating disturbance. The results of these studies has recently been analyzed and summarized.[16] This review located more than fifty studies in which the effectiveness of some thirty-eight different eating disorder prevention programs were tested. Elements of the different programs overlapped considerably, with most involving education about healthy and unhealthy eating behavior and attitudes, emphasis on the adverse consequences of eating disorders, enhancing coping skills, and teaching participants how to question and resist social and media pressures that lead to the internalization of the importance of extreme thinness. In all, 54 percent of the interventions report significant reductions in at least one reported risk factor for eating disorders (e.g., body dissatisfaction). However, the impact of these interventions appears to be moderate at best; whether the changes

16. E. Stice and H. Shaw, Eating disorder prevention programs: A meta-analytic review, *Psychological Bulletin* 130 (2004): 207.

persist over a long period of time remains unknown; and their ability to actually deter the onset of a severe eating disorder has not yet been established.

Much has been learned from the explosion of research in eating disorders in the past decade. It will be important to future efforts to develop even more rigorous approaches to isolating the many risk factors underlying unhealthy weight control methods and furthering knowledge of how these factors interact. Hopefully, the success of these efforts will translate into more effective preventative education and more effective treatments for those who suffer from eating disorders.

FURTHER READING

SUGGESTED READING FOR ADOLESCENTS

Body Changes

The Period Book: Everything You Don't Want to Ask (But Need to Know), by Karen Gravelle and Jennifer Gravelle. Illustrated by Debbie Palen. Harvard University Press, 2001.

The "What's Happening to My Body?" Book for Girls: A Growing Up Guide for Parents and Daughters, by Lynda Madaras with Area Madaras. Newmarket Press, 2001.

HELP! My Teacher Hates Me, by Meg Schneider. Workman Press, 1994.

Online Magazines for Girls

Girl Zone, www.girlzone.com.
New Moon, www.newmoon.org.

SUGGESTED READING FOR PARENTS

Dieting and Weight Issues

Fasting Girls: The History of Anorexia Nervosa, by Joan Jacobs Brumberg. Vintage, 2000.

Fat Talk: What Girls and Their Parents Say about Dieting, by Mimi Nichter. Harvard University Press, 2001.

How Did This Happen? A Practical Guide to Understanding Eating Disorders—for Teachers, Parents and Coaches. The Institute for Research and Education, 1999.

Stick Figure: A Diary of My Former Self, by Lori Gottlieb. Simon and Schuster, 2001.

When Girls Feel Fat: Helping Girls through Adolescence, by Sandra Susan Friedman. Firefly Books, 2000.

General Health

Healthy Teens, Body and Soul: A Parent's Complete Guide, by Andrea Marks and Betty Rothbard. Fireside, 2003.

The Teen Health Book: A Parent's Guide to Adolescent Health and Well-Being, by Ralph I. Lopez. Norton, 2003.

Divorce

Difficult Questions Kids Ask (And Are Too Afraid to Ask) about Divorce, by Meg Schneider. Fireside, 1996.

Good Parenting through Your Divorce: How to Recognize, Encourage, and Respond to Your Child's Feelings and Help Them Get Through Your Divorce, by Mary Ellen Hannibal. Marlowe, 2002.

What about the Kids? Raising Your Children before, during and after Divorce, by Judith Wallerstein. Hyperion, 2004.

Why Did You Have to Get a Divorce and Can We Get a Hamster? by Anthony E. Wolf. Farrar, Straus and Giroux, 1998.

Sex and Sexuality

The Big Talk: Talking to Your Child about Sex and Dating, by Laurie Langford. Wiley, 1998.

From Diapers to Dating: A Parent's Guide to Raising Sexually Healthy Children, by Debra W. Haffner. Newmarket, 2000.

Sex and Sensibility: The Thinking Parent's Guide to Talking Sense about Sex, by Deborah Roffman. Perseus, 2001.

General

I Can't Believe You Went Through My Stuff! How to Give Your Teens the Privacy They Crave and the Guidance They Need, by Peter Sheras with Andrea Thompson. Fireside, 2004.

Get Out of My Life—But First Could You Drive Me and Cheryl to the Mall? A Parent's Guide to the New Teenager, by Anthony E. Wolf. Farrar, Straus and Giroux, 2002.

Staying Connected to Your Teenager: How to Keep Them Talking to You and How to Hear What They're Really Saying, by Michael Riera. Perseus, 2003.

Uncommon Sense for Parents of Teenagers, by Michael Riera. Celestial Arts, 2004.

APPENDIX

BMI Charts

These growth charts give percentiles in the population for a wide range of the body mass index (BMI), which is a measure of body mass taking into account a person's height and weight. The following is a generally accepted interpretation of the meaning of variations in the body mass index.

A value below 20 indicates a lean BMI, which means that you have a low amount of body fat. If you are an athlete, this can be desirable. If you are not an athlete, a lean BMI can indicate that your weight may be too low, which may lower your immunity. If your BMI and body weight are low, you should consider gaining weight through good diet and exercise habits to increase your muscle mass.

A BMI between 20 and 22 indicates a healthy amount of body fat, which is associated with living longest and the lowest incidence of serious illness. Coincidentally, this ratio is what many individuals perceive to be the most aesthetically attractive. However, it is important to note that a BMI between 22 and 25 is still considered an acceptable range and is associated with good health.

A BMI between 25 and 30 may be considered "hefty" by some. Lowering weight by changing the diet and increasing exercise can have personal and health benefits.

A BMI over 30 indicates an unhealthy condition, putting you at risk for heart disease, diabetes, high blood pressure, gallbladder disease, and some cancers.

CDC Growth Charts: United States

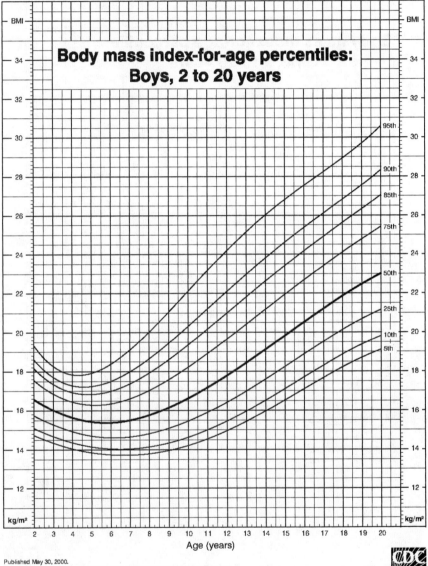

Body mass index-for-age percentiles: Boys, 2 to 20 years

Age (years)

Published May 30, 2000.
SOURCE: Developed by the National Center for Health Statistics in collaboration with
the National Center for Chronic Disease Prevention and Health Promotion (2000).

SAFER · HEALTHIER · PEOPLE™

CDC Growth Charts: United States

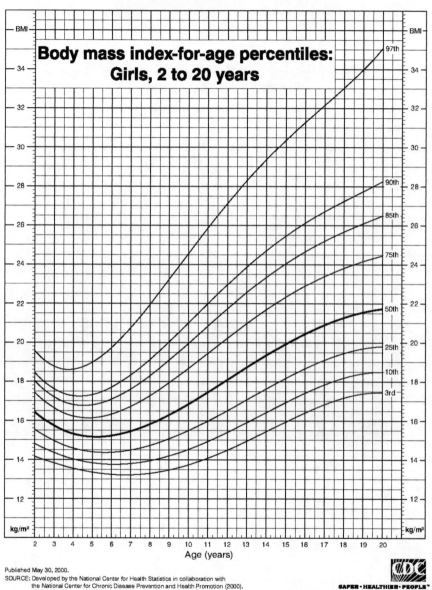

Body mass index-for-age percentiles:
Girls, 2 to 20 years

Published May 30, 2000.
SOURCE: Developed by the National Center for Health Statistics in collaboration with
   the National Center for Chronic Disease Prevention and Health Promotion (2000).

REFERENCES

Bulik, C., et al. Eating disorders and antecedent anxiety disorders: A controlled study. *Acta Psychiatrica Scandanavica* 96 (1997): 101–107.

Bulik, C. M., P. F. Sullivan, T. Wade, et al. Twin studies of eating disorders: A review. *International Journal of Eating Disorders* 27 (2000): 1–20.

Bulik, C., P. F. Sullivan, T. E. Weltzin, et al. Temperament in eating disorders. *International Journal of Eating Disorders* 17 (1995): 251–261.

Fairburn, C., Z. Cooper, H. A. Doll, et al. Risk factors for anorexia nervosa: Three integrated case-control comparisons. *Archives of General Psychiatry* 56 (1999): 468–476.

French, S. A., C. L. Perry, G. R. Leon, et al. Dieting behaviors and weight change history in female adolescents. *Health Psychology* 14 (1995): 548–555.

Johnson, J. G., P. Cohen, L. Kotler, et al. Psychiatric disorders associated with risk for the development of eating disorders during adolescence and early adulthood. *Journal of Consulting and Clinical Psychology* 70 (2002): 1119–1128.

Killen, J., et al. Weight concerns influence the development of eating disorders. *Journal of Clinical and Consulting Psychology* 64 (1996): 936–940.

Klump, K., C. M. Bulik, C. Pollice, et al. Temperament and character in women with eating disorders. *Journal of Nervous and Mental Disease* 188 (2000): 559–567.

Klump, K., W. Kaye, and M. Strober. The evolving genetic foundations of eating disorders. *Psychiatric Clinics of North America* 24 (2001): 215–225.

Krowchuk, D. P., S. R. Kreiter, C. R. Woods, et al. Problem dieting behaviors among young adolescents. *Archives of Pediatric Medicine* 152 (1998): 884–888.

Lewinsohn, P. M., H. Hops, R. E. Roberts, et al. Adolescent psychopathology: I. Prevalence and incidence of depression and other DSM-III-R disorders in high school students. *Journal of Abnormal Psychology* 102 (1993): 133–144.

Middleman, A. B., I. Vazquez, and R. H. DuRant. Eating patterns, physical activity, and attempts to change weight among adolescents. *Journal of Adolescent Health* 22 (1998): 37–42.

Paxton, S., et al. Friendship clique and peer influences on body image concerns, dietary restraint, extreme weight-loss behaviors, and binge eating in adolescent girls. *Journal of Abnormal Psychology* 108 (1999): 255–266.

Serdula, M. K., M. E. Collins, D. F. Williamson, et al. Weight control practices of U.S. adolescents and adults. *Annals of Internal Medicine* 119 (1993): 667–671.

Stice, E. Risk factors for body dissatisfaction in adolescent girls: A longitudinal investigation. *Developmental Psychology* 38 (2002): 669–678.

Stice, E. Risk and maintenance factors for eating pathology: A meta-analytic review. *Psychological Bulletin* 128 (2002): 825–848.

Stice, E., C. Hayward, R. P. Cameron, et al. Body-image and eating disturbances predict onset of depression among female adolescents. *Journal of Abnormal Psychology* 109 (2000): 438–444.

Stice, E., K. Presnell, and D. Spangler. Risk factors for binge eating onset in adolescent girls: A two-year prospective investigation. *Health Psychology* 21 (2002): 131–138.

Stice, E., and H. Shaw. Eating disorder prevention programs: A meta-analysis. *Psychological Bulletin* 130 (2004): 207–227.

Story, M., et al. Demographic and risk factors associated with chronic dieting in adolescents. *American Journal of Diseases in Childhood* 145 (1991): 994–998.

Strober, M., R. Freeman, C. Lampert, et al. Controlled family study of anorexia nervosa and bulimia nervosa: Evidence of shared liability and transmission of partial syndromes. *American Journal of Psychiatry* 157 (2000): 393–401.

INDEX